Policing Sex Crimes

THE APPLIED CRIMINOLOGY
ACROSS THE GLOBE SERIES

Series Editor

Kimberly A. McCabe, University of Lynchburg, mccabe@lynchburg.edu

Crime and safety continue to be among the top issues facing the global world, and the discipline of applied criminology addresses those issues. *The Applied Criminology across the Globe* series is designed to address the ever-growing need for current and accurate information on a variety of subjects as related to applied criminology. The books in this series provide the readers with monographs that are able to inform and educate individuals on crime and criminal behaviors.

Books in the Series

Policing and Public Trust: Exposing the Inner Uniform, by Eccy de Jonge. 2020.

The Crisis in America's Criminal Courts: Improving Criminal Justice Outcomes by Transforming Decision-Making, by William R. Kelly. 2021.

Sex Trafficking of Children Online: Modern Slavery in Cyberspace, by Beatriz Susana Uitts. 2022.

Policing Sex Crimes, by Dale Spencer and Rosemary Ricciardelli. 2022.

Policing Sex Crimes

Dale Spencer
Rosemary Ricciardelli

ROWMAN & LITTLEFIELD
Lanham • Boulder • New York • London

Published by Rowman & Littlefield
An imprint of The Rowman & Littlefield Publishing Group, Inc.
4501 Forbes Boulevard, Suite 200, Lanham, Maryland 20706
www.rowman.com

86-90 Paul Street, London EC2A 4NE, United Kingdom

Ricciardelli, R., D. C. Spencer, and A. Dodge. 2021. "'Society Wants to See a True Victim': Police Interpretations of Victims of Sexual Violence." *Feminist Criminology* 16 (2): 216–35.
Spencer, D., R. Ricciardelli, D. Ballucci, and K. Walby. 2019. "Cynicism, Dirty Work, and Policing Sex Crimes." *Policing: An International Journal* 43 (1): 151–65.
Dodge, A., D. Spencer, R. Ricciardelli, and D. Ballucci. 2019. "'This Isn't Your Father's Police Force': Digital Evidence in Sexual Assault Investigations." *Australian and New Zealand Journal of Criminology* 52 (4): 499–515.
Reprinted from Grace, A., R. Ricciardelli, D. Spencer, and D. Ballucci. 2019. "Collaborative Policing: Networked Responses to Child Victims of Sex Crimes." *Child Abuse & Neglect* 93: 197–207, with permission from Elsevier.

British Library Cataloguing in Publication Information Available

Library of Congress Cataloging-in-Publication Data
Names: Spencer, Dale C., 1979– author. | Ricciardelli, Rose, 1979– author.
Title: Policing sex crimes / Dale Spencer, Rosemary Ricciardelli.
Description: Lanham, Maryland: Rowman & Littlefield Publishing Group, [2022] | Series: Applied criminology across the globe | Includes bibliographical references and index. | Summary: "Unique in its approach, Policing Sex Crimes probes the investigations of sex crimes from the perspectives of investigators"—Provided by publisher.
Identifiers: LCCN 2022012264 (print) | LCCN 2022012265 (ebook) | ISBN 9781538159484 (cloth) | ISBN 9781538159491 (epub) | ISBN 9781538159507 (paper)
Subjects: LCSH: Sex crimes. | Sex and law.
Classification: LCC HV6556 .S65 2022 (print) | LCC HV6556 (ebook) | DDC 364.15/3—dc23/eng/20220622
LC record available at https://lccn.loc.gov/2022012264
LC ebook record available at https://lccn.loc.gov/2022012265

To all the sex crime investigators who took time out from their busy schedules to participate in this research

Contents

Acknowledgments

We would like to thank the following research assistants who helped us at various points in the data collection and analyses phases of this research project: James Liles, Anita Grace, and Joshua Hruschka. We are deeply grateful to Alexa Dodge for her thoughtful reflections and assistance at all stages of research for this book. Thanks to Dale Ballucci for her many contributions to this research. A special thanks to our friends, colleagues, and mentors who encouraged and supported us along the way. Finally, writing a book is no small task, and as such, we thank our respective families for giving us the time and space to write *Policing Sex Crimes*.

Sections of this book were published in the following publications:

1. Ricciardelli, R., D. C. Spencer, and A. Dodge. 2021. "'Society Wants to See a True Victim': Police Interpretations of Victims of Sexual Violence." *Feminist Criminology* 16 (2): 216–35.
2. Spencer, D., R. Ricciardelli, D. Ballucci, and K. Walby. 2019. "Cynicism, Dirty Work, and Policing Sex Crimes." *Policing: An International Journal* 43 (1): 151–65.
3. Grace, A., R. Ricciardelli, D. Spencer, and D. Ballucci. 2019. "Collaborative Policing: Networked Responses to Child Victims of Sex Crimes." *Child Abuse & Neglect* 93:197–207.
4. Dodge, A., D. Spencer, R. Ricciardelli, and D. Ballucci. 2019. "'This Isn't Your Father's Police Force': Digital Evidence in Sexual Assault Investigations." *Australian and New Zealand Journal of Criminology* 52 (4): 499–515.

Chapter 1

Introduction

Technological developments since the early 1990s challenge traditional conceptions of policing, as police work has become reoriented to a digitized world where life and crime are thoroughly technosocial (referring to how some individuals are more outspoken or active online than in person; Blakemore 2012, 16; boyd 2010). Traditional crimes, as well as emergent criminal activities, characterize this new era for policing. The policing of online environments and digital communication technologies involves challenges that require particular types of expertise, beyond advanced computer literacy and skills, such as navigating the darknet (Martin 2018) and acquiring an intimate familiarity with the ever-changing online landscape and associated manners of criminal activity.

Simultaneously, sexual violence and harassment are continuously evolving in modern society with innovations in digital communication technologies and the internet. In response, police face additional challenges that include remaining up to date on technologies, technical training, and deep social media awareness. Such a skill set is required for policing online environments, which involves managing, assessing, and categorizing a large quantity of digital evidence (e.g., photographs, videos, social media logs), as well as modernizing the resources (e.g., human and material) and facilities (e.g., equipment, technologies) required to investigate technological or digital evidence. Police must negotiate the complexity of cases that include both online and in-person elements of harm, and as such, investigations of sexual violence often require cooperation between cybercrime or internet child exploitation units and sexual assault and child abuse units. Moreover, police handle cases that involve suspects and complainants located in different geographical areas, which require collaboration with a second police service, and their technological needs, too, must be met. In addition, police must understand the harms caused by online sexual violence and responding to cases that rely on foreign technology or social media companies' cooperation.

Researchers note various shortcomings in the criminal justice response to sexual violence, some tied to technology and capacity (e.g., Powell and Henry 2018; Henry and Powell 2015), others tied to victim experiences (e.g., Javaid 2020), and some related to allegations of sexual assault (e.g., McMillan 2018; Norton and Grant, 2008). Thus, unsurprisingly, sexual assault remains one of the most underreported violent crimes, and victims who do report often express dissatisfaction with the response they receive (Carbone-Lopez, Slocum, and Kruttschnitt 2016; Murphy 2015). Legal reforms may also have unanticipated consequences that intensify select shortcomings (Chesney-Lind 2002; Corrigan 2013; Finley 1989), and these reforms are often most advantageous to those who fit within the confines of the "ideal victim," for instance, a clearly innocent child (Christie 1986). Across disciplines, scholars also suggest victims' needs are often disregarded in the law, and the individualized nature of their criminal cases leaves little opportunity for addressing systemic issues in the legal process (Maier 2008; Ullman and Townsend 2007). Within the landscape of these shortcomings and the positionality of diverse actors, in *Policing Sex Crimes* we offer an overview of the affordances and difficulties of investigating and responding to sex crimes in contemporary digital society.

The simplest to most complex sex crimes investigations can (and often do) have a digital component. The digital society within which we live creates a number of evidence obstacles and inter- and intraorganizational challenges for police in investigations of sex offenses and in relation to victims of sex crimes. In response, we begin the book by elucidating laws defining sex crimes across international contexts and examine how nation states have responded to digital sex crimes and related digital communication technologies via laws, policies, and practices. Next, we document the effects of digital sex crimes on the policing profession and the broader police organizations in which sex crime investigators work. Before concluding with recommendations and suggestions, we explore how police officers interpret victims and the challenges victims face achieving justice in the wake of sexual victimization.

WHY DO POLICE APPROACHES
TO SEX CRIMES MATTER?

Numerous scholars have shown the role of police in the overall shortcomings of criminal justice responses to sexual violence (Jordan 2008; Koster et al. 2016; Perrin 2017). Victims of sexual violence continue to feel blamed, shamed, or doubted by police when they report sexual assaults (Jordan 2001; Mulla 2014), and researchers report that police rely on stereotypes about sexual violence when assessing complainants' reports (Johnson 2015; Sheehy 2012). For example, Page (2007) found in her survey of police officers in the southeast United States that an overwhelming majority of officers believed any woman can be raped, a small portion were unlikely to believe a woman who reported being raped by her husband, and a significant portion were unlikely to believe a sex worker who claimed to be raped. In addition, officers with higher levels of education were less likely to endorse rape myths. In their interviews with Los Angeles Police Department and Los Angeles Sheriff's Department detectives, Spohn and Tellis (2012) found that officers either deployed an "innocent until guilty" or "guilty until innocent" approach. Officers deploying the former approach believed victims' allegations in both stranger and non-stranger sexual assault cases. Officers deploying the latter scheme, "guilty until innocent," did not take non-stranger rape as seriously as stranger rape. Elsewhere, Maier (2014) has demonstrated that law enforcement's treatment of victims is contingent on the perceived credibility of the victim's statement. As such, victims may feel and too often are revictimized by the criminal justice and legal systems.

In Canada and the United States, much attention has been paid to how shortcomings manifest, specifically in the form of "unfounded rates"—the label police apply to cases indicating that "the investigating officer does not believe a crime was attempted or occurred" (Butt 2017, 1; Spohn and Tellis 2012). While many police organizations have benefited from training and investigative policy updates regarding sexual assault, the unfounded rates for sexual violence are drastically higher than for other crimes and inconsistent across regions (Benoit et al. 2015; Light and Ruebsaat 2006). One of the reasons posited for the inconsistency is the role of police culture (Gregory and Lees 1999).

Police culture refers to a diverse, rather than singular, set of informal systems within police organizations that guide officers' conduct through their identification with, and preservation of, general attitudes/beliefs about the occupational work (Chan 1996; Goldsmith 1990; Paoline 2003). Policing scholars have documented differences among diverse police cultures, illustrating their dynamic nature and plurality (Chan 1997; Manning, 2007). Cultures vary both between (by service) and within police services, by unit, department, and shift. Despite the variation in police cultures, their existence marks a distinction between the formal rules of the organization and what guides officer behavior in practice. The main components of traditional police culture include the perception of danger on duty (Waddington 1999), solidarity among police officers (Chan 1997; Chan, Devery, and Doran 2003; Paoline 2003), a sense of mission (Manning 1977; Waddington 1999), and cynicism (Caplan 2003; Niederhoffer 1967). Campeau (2015), however, argues that police culture has recently changed due to the increased accountability and public visibility of both police organizations and individual officers. In her Canadian case study, she found that oversight has decreased the prevalence of "maintaining secrecy" and upholding the "blue wall of silence"—oft-cited elements of traditional police culture. Campeau (2015) posits that officers attempt to avoid crime-fighting initiatives in an effort to avoid scrutiny given the substantial increase in police visibility.

Contemporary views of police culture confirm that it is dynamic and amenable to change through a number of different factors. For example, varying mandates between police organizations reveal cultural difference at an organizational level (Goldsmith 1990; Paoline 2003). Similarly, officer rank affects police culture, as there are significant cultural variations between patrolling police officers, specialized units, and senior police officials (Farkas and Manning 1997; Reuss-Ianni 2011). As a result of their complex and ever-changing role, police organizations continue to challenge traditional conceptualizations of police culture through their partnerships with community organizations and reorientation toward service operations and assisting victims of crime. Policing scholars challenge the notion that police culture is monolithic and recognize that there may even be coexisting cultures (Campeau 2015; Loftus 2008, 2010), some of which are oriented and sensitive to the plight of victims of crime, especially in relation to sexual assault and internet child exploitation. Such alternative cultures may give rise to inclusive masculinities and gender performances that are characterized by greater care and concern for victims of all types.

Said reorientation, combined with greater visibility and reflexivity among police officers, signals a number of questions that animate *Policing Sex Crimes*. In this book, we probe how police investigators understand the policing of sex crimes and the many associated nuances. We also ponder how police officers judge the "viability" of sexual assault cases—the many technical realities impacting a case outcome—and how their judgments are influenced by the lens of their experience watching cases flounder in court. For example, might officers be wrongly labeling cases as unfounded, due to their knowledge of outmoded courtroom practices that fail to unpack the nuanced truths of sexual violence, and thus rarely result in conviction? If so, are police wrongly labeling such cases due to courtroom practices or, rather, due to their own shortcomings or those internal to the service? This is one of the many systemic relationships carefully examined in *Policing Sex Crimes*. Responding to gaps in the literature and understanding tied to policing in our culturally evolving and digitizing society, throughout the pages we unpack how police interpret broader criminal justice responses to sex crimes.

CONCEPTUAL TERRAIN AND LINES OF INQUIRY

In this book, we are not guided by a singular overarching theoretical framework; rather, we stitch together a constellation of concepts to make sense of sex crime investigations and investigators. Our conceptual framework consists of, among other things, "digital assemblages," "police culture," "ideal victim," and "networked policing" that function as a map of how all of the policing sex crime literature works together and offers a lens for understanding police investigations of sex crimes (cf. Collins and Stockton 2018). Such concepts, like digital assemblages and dirty work, are articulated to understand digital policing from the standpoint of police officers and their perspectives on sex crimes. Concomitantly, we engage with enduring concepts in the sociology of policing, like police culture and networked policing, to make sense of long-standing issues in policing and as a way of explaining the practices described by officers and the relationships forged with publics and other organizations.

That said, such concepts are, like all concepts, positioned in time and are attempts at apprehending the experiences and practices of others. We recognize that such interpretations of phenomena through concepts are attempts at fixing or apprehending the chaos and complexities of policing investigations, respectively. By engaging with sex laws and technology, and forming and utilizing concepts to understand policing sex crimes, we are trying to recognize the conditions under which such concepts can be understood and situated. We demonstrate how such concepts relate to each other and can be understood in relation to each other within the policing of sex crimes. Such a careful approach to concept formation and utilization is part of an overarching approach that is both appreciative and critical, thereby pointing simultaneously to the strengths and changes in policing sex crimes, as well as the enduringly negative aspects of sex crime investigations that disenfranchise and revictimize survivors.

Drawing from prison scholarship, particularly that of Alison Liebling and her colleagues (1999, 76), who have used appreciative inquiry in the study of prison environments, we build our appreciative position, which "can be a more creative and future-oriented process than the type of critical evaluation often carried out in prison[-related research]." To this end, we took an appreciative approach, starting by recognizing that any research (particularly that focused on such a delicate and scrutinized area of investigation) can leave a service (and unit) vulnerable and susceptible to additional scrutiny. Thus, we started by appreciating the practices in place and the efforts toward policing of sex crimes that had been established, rather than approaching with an entirely critical lens that suggested power relationships were always at play and policies were ambiguous in intention. We used appreciative inquiry, in that we approached criticalness within the context of the police service unit, and with readiness to find positive ways to build on or make change (Hammond 1998; Liebling 1999, 2001). We learned not only procedures but also why (and how) the procedures had come to be in place—legally, practically, and professionally. We paid close attention to how police service providers informed us of the occupational skills and challenges and how practices and policies were described, and we then tried to determine the grassroots of challenges as well as the reasons some policies were so well adapted and accepted. Using appreciative inquiry left us able to work collaboratively with police services across Canada and encouraged us to maintain a positive lens that gave credit where credit was due but also had space for critique when appropriate. As such, we could draw attention to challenges and gaps in knowledge, as well as attention to all that was done well or plans for future developments to support case construction and evidence processing. Our focus was on appreciation, not deficiencies.

Beyond appreciative inquiry, our approach to understanding police investigations of sex crimes is critical in orientation. Principally, this is to say that we offer a critique of not only policing practices that lead to destructive outcomes for victims but also the broader organizational context that police operate and their relationship to institutions beyond policing. Such a form of critique is measured by a broader consideration of the legal *and* technological terrain under which sex crime investigators work and our appreciative lens.

METHODS

We conducted case studies with ten police service organizations across Canada. These organizations were selected to provide a "coast-to-coast-to-coast" national representation of the different landscapes in the country, including suburban and urban areas. That is, the corresponding cities in this study reflect the diverse challenges to policing sex crimes in urban and rural Canada and in terms of their specific approaches to adult, child, and youth victims. We included four large cities (more than five hundred thousand residents), three mid-sized cities (between two hundred thousand and five hundred thousand residents), and three smaller cities (less than two hundred thousand residents) whose police services are also responsible for the surrounding areas. We initially conducted a pilot case study with sex crime victim-related service units to explore the main issues related to policing sex crimes across age categories (child, youth, and adult) and the types of units created to investigate and respond to various types of sex crimes.

Using a purposive sampling strategy (see Creswell 2012; Patton 2001), we chose participating police service organizations on the basis that they satisfied two criteria: (1) the police organization has one or more specialized units that respond to sex crimes that are separate from frontline officers; (2) the organization is embedded in an urban setting, as opposed to rural, because it is thus more likely to have dedicated units responding to sex crimes. We brokered access to the participating police organizations through e-mail and follow-up phone conversations with key gatekeepers to the respective organizations.

In addition to a pilot case study conducted with a police service organization in March 2014, we conducted case studies with nine police service organizations across Canada from November 2015 to June 2016. While the pilot case study police service organization had four victim-related units that pertain to the sexual victimization of children, youth, and adults, police organizations across Canada vary in the number of units they form to investigate and respond to sex crimes. The largest police service organization included in our study has eight different sex crime–related units, and the smallest police service had only one. As the size of the police organizations increases, the mandates of the individual sex crime units are narrower and specialized in relation to the type of victims to whom they respond.

We conducted seventy semistructured in-depth interviews and two focus groups with members of sex crime–related units in police service organizations. Thirty-three females and thirty-seven males—of whom thirty-one were between thirty-one and forty years of age, thirty-one were between forty-one and fifty, and eight were more than fifty years of age—participated in the study. In terms of ethnicity, most interviewees identified as white, and three identified as Indigenous or First Nations. Forty-three participants indicated that they are parents, and sixty-three were sworn members of their respective police service organizations (see table 1.1).

Table 1.1. Distributions of Participants' Occupational Role, Years of Experience, and Educational Profiles

Occupational Position			
Municipal Police Service	Royal Canadian Mounted Police	Branch of Canadian Government	
61	7	3	
Years of Experience			
Less than 5 years	5–10 years	10–20 years	20 plus years
3	9	46	13
Educational Attainment			
High School Diploma	College Diploma	University Degree	
13	13	42	

One or more of the research team members conducted semistructured in-depth interviews, elected because such interviews provide opportunities for the researcher to probe for details and depth when speaking with individual unit personnel on site. The interview guide consisted of forty-two intentionally wide-ranging open-ended questions. Interviews provided insights into how the officers and investigators understand sex crimes, their professions, specific offenders, and their experiences working with children, youth, and adult victims of sex crimes (see Flick 2014; Kvale and Brinkmann 2008; Marshall and Rossman 2011). We conducted focus groups with multiple members of sex crime units within two large police service organizations with follow-up interviews conducted with select members. The focus groups were intended to provide understanding of, first, the mandates of the individual sex crime units in these large organizations and, second, their perspectives regarding the challenges of investigating and responding to sex crimes. Interviews, however, were semistructured in nature and, thus, also followed the conversational path put forth by the participants. This process enabled the interviewer to probe areas of information beyond the guide and the participant to speak to what was most pertinently on their mind.

We conducted interviews with individual members of each sex crime unit; each was voice recorded and ranged from 30 to 150 minutes in length, with an average duration of 50 minutes. Research assistants transcribed interviews verbatim and assigned pseudonyms to all participants to ensure confidentiality.

We used QSR NVivo qualitative research software to assist with the compilation, organization, and coding of the interview and focus group transcripts. A member of the research team initially coded transcripts using open coding to identify theoretical, process, and attribute codes. Then, the research team met to create a list of all codes that had emerged, and through a process of codebook revision and recoding, we achieved consensus regarding the meaning of the codes and created a fulsome list of codes (Campbell et al. 2013; Carey, Morgan, and Oxtoby 1996). A second member of the research team then read and coded all transcripts in full using the full list of agreed upon themes (Charmaz 2006). More than eighty codes emerged from the interview and focus group data.

SIGNPOSTING THE NARRATIVE

Across societies, offenders are rarely met with the degree of contempt and hatred directed toward those suspected, accused, or convicted of sex crimes (Ricciardelli and Spencer 2017). Sex crimes—particularly those against innocent children—are met with contempt and, often, misunderstanding. In chapter 2, we reflect on how sex crimes are interpreted and defined internationally from a legal standpoint, as well as the ever-increasing forms of sex crimes related to digital communication technologies. We introduce the concept of digital assemblages, the construct guiding our approach to the relationship among police, digital technology, and sex crime investigations.

In chapter 3, we turn our attention to how there has been widespread acceptance of the need to digitize the policing of child pornography offenses yet much less attention paid to the role of digital evidence in other sex crime investigations. Digital evidence is now present in many (or arguably most) cases of sexual assault, and this infusion of evidence creates the need for new investigative tools and policing strategies. The growing importance of digital evidence in sex crime cases demonstrates the necessity of analyzing how police understand the potential capacity and pitfalls of gathering and using this evidence. Here, in chapter 3, we demonstrate that the nature of sex crime investigations has radically changed with the introduction and use of digital technologies. We show that digital evidence has become ubiquitous in this area, resulting in notable changes to the training and skill set required of police, leaving us to argue that the increasingly digital nature of sex crime investigations requires "digital policing."

In chapter 4, we recognize that, despite attempts to rectify the injustices victims of sexual violence experience within the criminal justice system, unfounded rates for sexual violence remain high, and many victims continue to feel disempowered and voiceless. In this context, police officers are torn between representing the voiceless and disempowered and protecting those who are falsely accused from the stigma of the sex offender label. In chapter 4, we seek to understand how police interpret and respond to child, youth, and adult victims of sex crimes. We unpack the range of interpretations of victims, explore if and how interpretations of victims translate into police perceptions of their interactions with victims, and examine police interpretations of the possible outcomes that can be offered in the investigation. We highlight the difficulties officers encounter as they strive to balance their occupational role with victims' needs. With this in mind, we argue that police interpretations of sexual violence and sexual violence victims are shaped by the officer's adherence to or rejection of understandings of the "ideal victim." In addition, we explore police interpretations of the obstacles to achieving justice in cases of sexual violence. Our findings demonstrate that the majority of officers are critical of the present criminal justice response to sexual violence and are doubtful of its ability to provide a semblance of justice to the majority of victims.

Next, in chapter 5, we direct our attention toward the rights of victims of crime as legislated in the United States and in Canadian provinces and territories such that victims have access to assistance services and programs including medical, social, family, and mental health supports. The responsibility for service provision, however, increasingly falls on police, although the actual therapeutic work takes place within community organizations. Given that practices relating to victim support have traditionally been considered the "soft" functions of policing—in contrast to "hard" functions of fighting crime and disorder—how policing roles are evolving in response and how police interact with the community agencies involved in victim support require empirical examination. In chapter 5, then, we examine police responses to child victims of sex crimes, recognizing that Canadian and US police agencies are increasingly required to work collaboratively with community organizations, a movement that generates benefits and challenges for police. We unpack the processes by which traditional police roles and responsibilities are simultaneously entrenched and challenged through collaborative projects with child victim–oriented community partners and through the shift in orientation toward victims of crime. Significantly, police identify child advocacy centers as sites of best practice in police/community partnerships in response to child victims of sexual assault.

Chapter 6, the final empirical chapter, looks at how, now, digital evidence is infused in many (or arguably most) sex crime cases. This fact has refigured investigative tools, policing strategies, and sources of cynicism for those working in sex crime units. Although cynicism, both its sources and effects, is widely studied among scholars of policing, little is known about how police working in sex crime units experience, mitigate, and express cynicism. By examining sources of cynicism and emotional experiences, we reveal that officers in these units normalize organizational and intraorganizational sources of cynicism and experience traumatizing and emotionally draining realities of undertaking this form of "dirty work." We show that officer cynicism extends beyond criminalized individuals into organizational and operational aspects of their occupations and their lived experiences outside of work, which has implications for literature on police work, cynicism, and digital policing. In the final, concluding chapter we offer an overview of this book and recommendations for the future of digital policing of sex crimes.

Chapter 2

Sex Crimes, Law, and Technology

Criminal law in Canada, the United States, the United Kingdom, and Australia is often structured in similar ways, as the legal structures of these countries refer to each other when making decisions on how to structure specific elements of their legal codes. The academic literature on laws related to sexual behavior and sexual violence testifies to the phenomena of legal drift. For example, Frank and colleagues (2010) show how changes in national legal systems were reflected in the criminalization and regulation of sexual violence and sexual behavior and were affected by major global events such as World War II and grassroots movements advocating for certain reforms. Looking at the structures of criminal law on a comparative international scale, it can be gleaned that changes in crimes of sexual violence and sexual violence legislation have been dramatically affected by the digital networks that span the globe (Ebbe 2013, 4).

In this chapter, we primarily discuss two principal determining factors shaping investigations of and responses to sex crimes: law and technology. We refrain from using the term "crimes of sexual violence," which refers to the criminalization of nonconsensual sexual acts rather than the criminalization/regulation of consensual sex acts. We make this distinction because our focus is on police work, not a critical assessment of the criminalization of consensual acts. Police have to enforce the law and investigate acts that have been criminalized. We offer a comparison of *legal* responses to sexual violence as a means to reflect on the complex terrain sex crime police investigators navigate. We do so based on the fact that how a nation defines and structures their response to sex crimes matters for the delivery of criminal justice. In addition, we detail how the emergence of digital infrastructures, or as we refer to them here, digital assemblages, have intersected with criminal law in ways that, to varying degrees, reflect the nature of sex crimes.

LEGAL RESPONSES TO SEX CRIMES

In this section, we offer an overview of the various laws that have been created to respond to sex crimes. We are not concerned with how these laws came about; rather, we are interested in the scope and structure of sex crime laws in English-speaking countries. We have made the decision to address sex crime laws in the United Kingdom, the United States, Canada, and Australia because of the common genesis of these laws (starting in the United Kingdom) and the cross-fertilization of legal approaches to nonconsensual sexual(ized) behaviors that are deemed unacceptable. Such framing of legal responses to sex crimes matters insofar as they create the environment in which sex crime police investigators carry out their work and in terms of their ability to address sex crimes that are international in scope and effect.

In Canada, the country in which we collected the data, sexual offenses are largely divided into two main sections—part 5, "Sexual Offences, Public Morals, and Disorderly Conduct," and part 8, "Offences against the Person and Reputation." The structure is then broken down by who is being affected by the crime under these sections. In part 5, crimes are largely focused on those targeting persons under the age of sixteen or thirteen. This part begins with crimes such as sexual interference, including "sexual touching with a person under sixteen" or inviting a person under sixteen to engage in sexual touching. This is followed by "sexual exploitation" focused on offenses committed by individuals in a position of trust or authority toward a young person. In Canada, a "young person" is defined as "a person sixteen years of age or more but under the age of eighteen years." We use this definition to distinguish between adults (above eighteen) and children (under sixteen). Also included in this section are crimes such as "sexual exploitation of a person with a disability," "incest," "voyeurism," and "the publication of an intimate image without consent." For the purposes of review, both voyeurism and the publication of an intimate image without consent include cybercrime provisions that work to include the publication of intimate images online and use terminology such as "making available," "transmitting," and "copying" that can be used when referring to the circulation of intimate images online.

Part 5 of the criminal code also includes the subsection "Offences Tending to Corrupt Morals" that focuses on both the inclusion of the production and dissemination of "obscene materials" and "child pornography." For the purposes of the criminal code, obscene material is defined as "any publication a dominant characteristic of which is the undue exploitation of sex, or of sex and any one or more of the following subjects, namely, crime, horror, cruelty and violence." Additionally, child pornography is defined as

[a] photographic, film, video or other visual representation, whether or not it was made by electronic or mechanical means, (i) that shows a person who is or is depicted as being under the age of eighteen years and is engaged in or is depicted as engaged in explicit sexual activity, or (ii) the dominant characteristic of which is the depiction, for a sexual purpose, of a sexual organ or the anal region of a person under the age of eighteen years; (b) any written material, visual representation or audio recording that advocates or counsels sexual activity with a person under the age of eighteen years that would be an offence under this Act; (c) any written material whose dominant characteristic is the description, for a sexual purpose, of sexual activity with a person under the age of eighteen years that would be an offence under this Act; or (d) any audio recording that has as its dominant characteristic the description, presentation or representation, for a sexual purpose, of sexual activity with a person under the age of eighteen years that would be an offence under this Act.

This section of the criminal code focuses heavily on the topic of child pornography and includes provisions for making, distributing, possessing, and benefiting from child pornography. There are also specific provisions for how the pornography was made, and whether it was done in an aggravated fashion. The following section presents some of the key cybercrime provisions included in the Canadian Criminal Code—those surrounding the luring of children. Section 172, "Luring a Child," states the following:

Every person commits an offense who, by a means of telecommunication, communicates with (a) a person who is, or who the accused believes is, under the age of 18 years, for the purpose of facilitating the commission of an offense with respect to that person under subsection 153(1), section 155, 163.1, 170, 171 or 279.011 or subsection 279.02(2), 279.03(2), 286.1(2), 286.2(2) or 286.3(2); (b) a person who is, or who the accused believes is, under the age of 16 years, for the purpose of facilitating the commission of an offense under section 151 or 152, subsection 160(3) or 173(2) or section 271, 272, 273 or 280 with respect to that person; or (c) a person who is, or who the accused believes is, under the age of 14 years, for the purpose of facilitating the commission of an offense under section 281 with respect to that person.

The provisions here focus on the modern nature of digital crimes where the luring of children online has become of increasing concern, a topic on the Government of Canada website under their "crime and crime prevention" page. On the website, a specific page is dedicated to "cybercrime," and much of the focus of this page is child sexual exploitation. The website seeks to provide awareness about the issue of cybercrime in Canada and how cybercrime can be prevented, or at least reduced. Much of the imagery on the website is centered on children using devices—showing the impact that these laws surrounding "luring a child" are having on perceptions of what a cybersex crime looks like and who it targets.

Finally, part 5 of the criminal code finishes with a subsection on "disorderly conduct" that begins with a provision on the agreement or arrangements of sexual offenses committed toward a child; followed by provisions for "indecent acts," "exposure," and "nudity." In this section, the laws surrounding all manner of sexual offenses are detailed, importantly excluding sexual assault. Both the United States and the United Kingdom include all sexual offenses under one section, as we will show shortly. Canada, however, separates sexual assault and prostitution from all other sexual offenses, suggesting these crimes have come to occupy different spaces in the collective conscience of Canadians. Moving to part 8, we can see the ways sexual assault has been defined and how sexual assault has come to occupy a different legal space than other sexual offenses.

Part 8, "Offences against the Person and Reputation" outlines a wide range of laws dealing with everything from homicide, suicide, medical-assisted dying, assaults, kidnapping, prostitution, abortion, hate propaganda, and a long list of others. Of interest to sexual-related offenses are crimes including sexual assault, commodification of sexual activity, and administering a noxious substance. The section begins with the crime of "administering a noxious substance" that focuses on the administering of, or forcing another to take, a drug or poison. Although not inherently related to sexual offenses, in the Australian and the UK legal codes on sexual offenses, administering a noxious substance is outlined as an offense in the cases of attempting to commit some form of sexual assault. The Canadian code does not link this directly with sex crimes but, rather, leaves it open to multiple interpretations, and for use across criminality. The definition of "assault" used for sexual assaults includes little discernment as to what is the actual definition of "sexual assault." Sexual assaults are thus not differentiated between penetrative and nonpenetrative acts, as is the case in the United Kingdom, the United States, and Australia, which make clear distinctions between types of assault whether they be penetrative or not.

Following sexual assaults, the code moves into kidnapping and human trafficking, and finally to the commodification of sexual activity. In this section, sexual commodification focuses on the obtaining of services and is split into obtaining services from individuals older than eighteen and younger than eighteen. This section also includes provisions for material benefit from sexual services, procuring people for sexual services, and advertising sexual services. At one time the section contained provisions for venereal diseases and their transmission, but this has since been repealed.

Throughout the Criminal Code of Canada, there is reference to the cyber elements of sex crimes. Whereas in some sections of the code digital or online elements are not explicitly mentioned, we will show in chapter 3 that the overwhelming lion's share of sex crimes have digital/cyber components and digital evidence is part and parcel of the investigation. Next, we turn to the United States to see how sex crimes are defined and linked to federal and state legislation and specific responses to sex crimes.

The United States is governed by both national laws and state-based laws, and for the purposes of our review, and to be consistent with our review of the Canadian Criminal Code, we will only look at national-level legislation. In the United States, criminal code sexual offenses are contained in two sections—section 109 and section 110 under title 18, "Crimes and Criminal Procedure." Section 109 outlines the details of crimes under the heading of "Sexual Abuse" and includes sexual abuse, aggravated sexual abuse, and sexual abuse of a minor or ward. The law then focuses on the national registry of sex offenders with a great amount of detail surrounding sexual offenses committed against children. Much space is committed to the details surrounding the registry of sex offenders in the United States as a whole.

Section 110 then focuses on sexual exploitation and other forms of abuse toward children. This section includes provisions for sexual exploitation, human trafficking, child pornography, and cybercrimes relating to children. The United States focuses their cybercrime laws on sexual exploitation of minors, including article 2252B (detailing the use of "misleading domain names on the Internet") and 2252C (dealing with "misleading words or digital images on the Internet"). As well, the United States has specific provisions for their "CyberTipline" and the use of technical elements to combat child pornography. In this section of the book, we give space to the production of child pornography and all elements that surround such production, including the selling and buying of children; obtaining, distributing, and hosting content; and failures to report child abuse. Finally, there are specific provisions for mandatory restitution for child abuse and exploitation. Outside of these nationally recognized laws, all other sexual offenses are relegated to the state-level legal codes.

The United Kingdom is the only region in our review that has a specific act solely for sexual offenses—the Sexual Offences Act of 2003. The act is quite comprehensive and contains information on every type of sexual offense in the United Kingdom. The act starts with a list of four types of crimes based on sexual acts that can occur against adults, including rape, assault by penetration, sexual assault, and causing a person to engage in sexual activity without consent. Following this initial section on sexual assaults, sections 5 through 26 focus on all matter of child-related offenses: assault, child prostitution, abuses of position of trust, and a variety of crimes related to causing a child to engage in sexual acts including cybercrimes such as sexual grooming and having sexual communication with a child.

Following these child-related sexual offenses are crimes relating to "family relationships," such as incest. The legislation then moves into sections 30–44 that focus on positions of care, trust, and "people with a mental disorder." The Sexual Offences Act then contains sections 45–75 that deal with a wide variety of offenses moving from prostitution, voyeurism, exposure, incest with adult relatives, administering a substance, bestiality, and offenses that occur outside of the United Kingdom. The act evidences an attempt to contain all sexual-related offenses of any kind into one act and that planning has gone into its organization as a whole. This is quite different from the Canadian code and the US codes where sexual offenses fall under different sections and are grouped in with other types of offenses against the individual.

The Australian national legal code has very few provisions for sexual offenses as they explicitly have worked to have individual provinces be in total control of their legal codes. Therefore, in the national code there is a specific section, titled "Crimes against Australians," that details a variety of offenses, including sexual assault, perpetrated against Australians by citizens of other countries or while Australians are abroad. This also includes the international trafficking of children and the procuring of children for sexual acts while Australians are abroad.

To provide some detail on the structures of Australian criminal codes, we specifically focus on the sex crime laws of New South Wales as its structure was fairly representative of the other provinces. The New South Wales criminal code is structured similarly to Canada's and that of the United States. Part 3 is titled "Offences against the Person" of which division 10 is "Sexual Offences against Adults and Children." Subdivision 2 focuses on sexual assault and assault with intent to have sexual intercourse and includes provision for aggravated assault and for when the offender is married to the victim. This is followed by subdivisions 3 and 4 that focus on sexual touching and sexual acts. Subdivision 5 through 9 include specific provisions for sexual offenses against children. Subdivision 10 includes "grooming a child," which includes cybercrime provisions much like the other criminal codes we discussed earlier in the chapter.

Succeeding these sections are provisions regarding sexual offenses toward people with a "cognitive impairment" and young people under special care. This is followed by incest, bestiality, and then a "Miscellaneous" section that works as a catch-all for other circumstances not already mentioned and largely focuses on minors committing sexual offenses. Subdivisions 14 and 15 deal with prostitution and child prostitution, respectively. The final three sections of the code, 15A, 15B, and 15C, present legislation tied to child abuse material, voyeurism, and recording/distributing intimate images. These sections do not include any specific cybercrime provisions but, rather, reference the internet as part of the possible places where distribution, procuring, and possession can occur. The Australian criminal code has a similar structure to that in the United Kingdom, as it appears to be a well-thought-out act that holds all sexual offenses in one clear division. Unlike the UK legislation, however, the Australian appears under a generalized heading that contains many other types of offenses, including those that are not sexual in nature, which is similar to the Canadian legislation.

COMPARING LAWS AND CRIMINAL JUSTICE SYSTEMS

Comparing legal responses to crimes across national lines can help identify trends in criminal justice reform occurring both nationally and internationally, while also providing an important viewpoint on what the individual country in question values culturally and socially. Ebbe (2013, 7) looks to this practice of comparison across nations as a process that nations can use to learn, based on the practices of others, what mechanisms may work for overseeing criminalized individuals, specifically sex offenders however defined. We can also look to the international nature of modern crime as a reason to include comparative forms of analysis across nations; doing so further helps us understand how crimes are happening across borders, the responses different nations use, and how such responses impact the nature of policing sex crimes (Ebbe 2013, 4). Lastly, Ebbe (2013, 7) shows us that with cross-country criminal justice system comparison we can determine the grassroots movements, social control mechanisms, and political histories that all come to affect criminal law and how these can affect law in the country in question. To this end, unpacking the nuances around sex crime–related legislation across countries provides a space for identifying how sex crimes are evolving in society, and how different jurisdictions respond to this evolution, which is informed by unique histories, as countries strive to ensure public safety.

Chon and Clifford (2021), for example, examine prevalence rates of rape on an international level in conjunction with the legislation around rape laws to unpack how rape legislation affects rates of rape as they occur in those countries. In previous studies, Chon and Clifford (2021, 2) found a "significant positive relationship between gender equality and cross-national rates of reported rapes," which had originally been viewed as supportive of the "backlash hypothesis." The backlash hypothesis is a theory that seeks to explain the rising prevalence of rape in countries with more progressive laws and social norms regarding gender-based crime. The theory posits men would use sexual assault to reinforce women's inferior positions when women began to achieve higher socioeconomic status and gender equality in any given society

(245). Through their research, the authors found that, as rape laws changed to include more mechanisms to protect and value women in various circumstances, more rapes were being reported (245). Although the rape rate may appear as increasing, however, in comparison to findings in other countries, where rapes are largely going unreported (especially in places where marital rape is not recognized), we see that it is not actually that rape is occurring more frequently but, rather, that women feel as though they have more ability to report these events. Thus, changing legislation and offers of protection for victims has increased reporting of sexual assault, specifically rape.

In their research, Chon and Clifford (2021) examine legislation specifically in the United Kingdom, situating the United Kingdom as a basis for international comparison because the country stands out among other developed nations—its rape laws differ from others such as those in Canada and the United States quite drastically. As the authors show, "English common law considers rape to only include penile-vaginal intercourse and does not recognize male rape victims" (Chon and Clifford 2021, 246). Marital rape was criminalized in case law in 1991 and officially included in written law in 2003 in the United Kingdom, where approximately 45 percent of rapes occur between partners. Therefore, given the rates of marital rape, whether or not a country has a "marital rape clause" drastically impacts rape rates (247). Along with this, Chon and Clifford argue that "the comprehensiveness of the legal definition of rape may influence police officers' reactions to sexual assault," and as police officers are "gatekeepers to the criminal justice system," their discretionary decision-making power affects how rapes are reported, valued, and recorded (247). In the end, Chon and Clifford found that "countries with high rates of official rape often have comprehensive legal definitions of rape" and that these often include many types of sexual assault as being included under the heading of "rape crimes" (258).

Turning to the work of Cashman (2000), we see how sexual offense law is closely associated with gender politics on an international scale. As Cashman argues, "[t]he crime of rape is unique insofar as it defines deviant sexual activity and therefore establishes the limits and terms of normal heterosexual encounters and gender relations" (2000, 122). As Cashman evinces, rape law does not only have an impact on how rape is culturally understood, but the legislation also creates the parameters within which reform can occur to the law (123). Cashman points first to Canada, where "liberal legalism" has worked to impact the reform of rape laws over time (123). In the 1970s and 1980s, rape law became a point of controversy for women's groups in Canada, the United Kingdom, Australia, and the United States, with strong critiques arising about the definitions of rape (125). In Canada, inequality regarding culpability could not be justified in a liberal framework, and in 1985, new revised laws were enacted that focused on sexual assault provisions and moved away from this outdated and essentializing discourse of "rape."

Another way scholars have looked at cross-country comparisons of sexual offense law is regarding sex trafficking. Sex trafficking is one of the key areas where cybercrime provisions are evidence across trends in most countries that have implemented legal provisions targeting telecommunications devices such as cell phones, tablets, and computers. These legal provisions are still few and far between overall but show a clear movement toward the criminalization of telecommunications– and digital communications–based trafficking. In their work on trafficking and sexual exploitation, Jakobsson and Kotsadam (2011) examine prostitution/sex work and trafficking laws across Europe and North America to understand how these laws affect trafficking in those countries. They suggest that harsher laws on prostitution and trafficking would work to reduce trafficking (2011, 102). When comparing laws on prostitution and trafficking and the levels of trafficking occurring into those countries, they found that countries such as Canada that had made prostitution legal but procuring it illegal had mid-levels of trafficking, whereas countries such as Sweden and Norway that had harsh laws had the lowest levels of trafficking (102). They argue that, as countries enacted harsher laws on prostitution and trafficking, there was a correlation to lower levels of trafficking into the country. When we look to the United Kingdom, Canada, Australia, and the United States, we can see they have similar laws on prostitution and trafficking, which all fall under this mid-level approach Jakobsson and Kotsadam (2011) describe.

Frank and colleagues (2010, 868) analyze how sexual offense law reform is a part of a general worldwide trend toward changes to models of society. They argue that most penal codes separate sexual offenses into different forms of sex, but legislation often forms a coherent policy that is affected by public discourses surrounding sex and sex crime–related issues (869). They argue that, as world societies move toward individualized forms, the position of sex in society changed from procreation to recreation (870). As sex for procreation became less prevalent and sex for pleasure became more prevalent, consent became "the cardinal rule in sexual relations" (871). Consent, again, has a great effect on sexual offenses, and specifically those regarding spousal abuse, as sexual offenses were no longer viewed as being against public morality and the public good but, rather, as against the individual (872). Such a transition in ideologies and understanding means waves of reform began to occur around the globe that involved the criminalization of spousal sexual abuse. What Frank and colleagues focus on is that sexual offense law reform often occurs as part of global trends, which is why we see similar legal reform across nations within short time spans.

In their work on rape law, Daly and Bouhours (2010, 566) compared "police and court responses to rape" across Australia, Canada, England and Wales, Scotland, and the United States between 1970 and 2005 to analyze the handling of sexual assault cases across various forms of the criminal justice system. As they show, rape law reform arose in Australia and the United States in the 1970s with Canada closely following behind in the 1980s (576). The United Kingdom was the latest to join this movement toward reform with some minor amendments in the 1970s and 1980s, but full reform did not occur until 2003 (576). One of the large trends evidenced in sexual offense legal reform began in the United States in the 1980s with the introduction of rape shield laws "that restricted using evidence at trial about a victim's sexual history, elimination of the corroboration rule, and in some states, elimination of evidence of physical resistance" (577). This also included reform focused on changing the definitions of rape and to including male and married victims (577). In 1983, Canada instituted a comprehensive set of reforms that included all of those reforms seen in the United States over the next ten years. England followed behind these reforms in 2003 and included many of the same provisions while maintaining laws specifically pertaining to rape as differentiated from sexual assault. Finally, Scotland introduced some reforms, but also appeared to move in the opposite direction with the allowance of greater "sexual history and character evidence" and only recognizing female victims of rape (578). As Daly and Bouhours found, these countries often followed one another in terms of legal reform with England and Scotland being the outliers in terms of sexual offense law reform.

We have shown here, in a very preliminary review, that much of the literature that works to compare sexual offense law across these nations focuses on how legal reform has occurred and how this reform has affected various aspects of sexual offenses in those countries. McMahon-Howard (2011) speaks to the ways sexual offense legal reform has occurred in these countries and how the controversial nature of these reforms has impacted how legislations are put into practice. She demonstrates that when partial reforms would occur earlier, this actually led to a lower likelihood of more controversial reforms later on (2011, 428). She indicates that there was a positive correlation between partial rape law reform and social movements that fought for greater reforms, but that this did not lead to the acceptance of greater reforms in the law later on and often led to a hesitance to enact greater reforms (429). Perhaps a lack in reform is due to countries (or societies) seeing the direct effects of previous reforms and therefore not believing in their overall efficacy.

Overall, we can see that countries move in waves to enact legal reforms regarding sexual offenses and that these are tied to the interconnectedness of the societies enacting those reforms. As societies have greater international connection, they seem to be more likely to have similar legal codes. Therefore, the nations in question—Canada, the United States, the United Kingdom, and Australia—have close international social connections, with the flow of individuals between these nations and the sharing of information being quite fluid. It should come as no surprise, then, that much of these countries' law regarding sexual offenses are quite similar. We see minor differences in definitions and punishments based on the particular values of the nation in question, but overall, these nations tend to mirror one another in their legal responses to sexual offenses. Regarding these nations' cybercrime provisions, it appears as though only some reforms have begun to arise since the mid-2000s, but these trends will most likely continue as we see active initiatives to inform people of these crimes. There is not necessarily a need for specific cyber-related legislation around sex crimes that occur online; for instance, voyeurism laws apply to cases using digital technology without necessarily requiring re-envisioning. With technology, however, come new modes and measures for engaging in sex-related crimes that create an ever-changing landscape for the policing of sex crimes. Such an evolving landscape then requires provisions to respond to new and emergent sex crimes as they occur online. As crime continues to occur on an international scale, using digital communication technologies allows for the enactment of specific provisions, particularly those targeting these offenses. In the next section, we outline our approach to digital technologies.

DIGITAL ASSEMBLAGES AND SEX CRIMES

Within the science and technology studies literature, there are enduring debates concerning the association between humans and technology. Here, we only engage with this debate as a way of situating our approach to technology and to how police investigators engage with the broader digital infrastructure within which they must investigate and respond to sex crimes. There are three main prevailing positions within the literature that we will summarize in this section: the conventional view of culture and technology, the view that technology must be understood within its own context, and technologies articulation.

The first, most widespread position is the conventional view of culture and technology. In this "modern" world(view), technologies are not human, and human beings are not technologies (Latour 2012). Such a position interprets technology as distinct from humans. These debates are based on two positions, that technology is neutral and merely a tool, reflecting the instrumentalist view, or the deterministic view, where technology controls human behavior (Feenberg 2002). Regarding the dominant instrumentalist view, technology is subservient to *values* founded in various social domains. To be instrumental means that technology is only contingently related to the substantive values it serves. Technology is indifferent to culture and politics and only employed to the variety of ends technology can be engaged to achieve.

The deterministic view, or substantive theory of technology, asserts that technology is an independent cultural force that dominates all traditional and/or competing values. This view claims that the deployment of technology modifies humanity and nature in consequential ways that overshadow the goals and benefits derived from its deployment. This perspective, most associated with Martin Heidegger (1977), claims that technology establishes a new cultural system that reorganizes the entire social world as an object of control and rationalization. Such a system of control is categorized by an extensive interrelationship that overwhelms every pretechnological enclave and forms the entirety of social life. Such an overwhelming system is dedicated to total instrumentalization of society without escape. The substantive side of this position is based on the assertion that technology is not merely a means but, rather, has become an environment and a way of life (Heidegger 1977; Virilio 1991, 2008). Technology has had a fundamental influence on society. Our interactions with technology have continually changed as our technologies have developed.

There are several difficulties with both the instrumental and deterministic view of technology. First, such polar views of technology lead to unending disputes regarding whether technologies are controlling humans or whether humans completely control technologies. Second, in both perspectives, technologies are discrete objects with identities of their own that can be analyzed by themselves in isolation. Any troubling of the relationship between humans and technology is regarded with skepticism. How technology is becoming more human or how humans are becoming more technological through implants is beyond these conceptions; humans are never embedded in technological networks or vice versa. Third, these perspectives also lack nuance as matters of degree of determinism in both directions are not recognized.

The second, less prominent, position on the human technology relationship asserts that, to understand this relationship, technologies must be understood in their context. Technologies are not separate from their context, and nor are human beings (Wise 2005). Scholars here argue that we cannot analyze a technology in isolation as technology is always in use within a context. The technology-human relationship is understood in situ, rather than in the abstract, and that human beings and technologies constrain each other. Tools provide both capacities and limitations for human action, and users are responsible for taking advantage of capacities and overcoming limitations in everyday use (Howard 2003). Technology is neither absolutely determined by humans, nor does technology determine or control human behavior. Moreover, technology and humans can be both embedded *and* disembedded. Against the backdrop of twenty-first-century digital technologies, individual citizens are never, thanks to global satellite surveillance, for example, completely disembedded from technology. We are always already in relation to technologies and vice versa.

The third position, which forms the basis of the approach we develop here, is that of articulation. The concept of articulation is based on the notion that different elements can be connected, or articulated, or disconnected to create unities or identities (Hall 1986; Slack 1989; Slack, Miller, and Doak 1993). Slack (1989, 329) avers that the concept of context is a "substantial theoretical problem" because analysts inescapably define the relevant context differently. In response to this problem, Slack offers a model of articulation that views the context as constitutive of the technology and the user/human. Technologies, then, cannot be disembedded. Within this approach, the "unities forged and broken in this expanded universe are not simply physical objects, such as trucks, but complex connections of elements that are themselves articulations. These elements or identities might be social practices, discursive statements, ideological positions, social forces, or social groups. . . . The unities they form can be made up of any combination of elements" (331).

Articulations are unambiguously historically contingent. Any articulations are made, sustained, transformed, and unmade in specific material practices. To articulate, to make or break connections between objects, between ideas, between objects and ideas, takes power: "Power not only draws and redraws the connections among the disparate elements within which identities are designated, but in the process, power designates certain of these articulations as dominant and others as subordinate" (Slack 1989, 333). Technology is a continuous series of articulations, as is being human.

What the concept of articulation allows for is an engagement with the non-modernist value of linkages, associations, and heterogeneous assemblages of bodies, technologies, and knowledges that make up the everyday (Latour 2004). Specifically, such an approach to technology and humans aligns with Latour's (1999, 2004, 2012) approach to networks and assemblages, chains of weaker and stronger association that cut through technology and society. By adopting this approach, we can engage with the material interventions of matter and the human organism world in how agency and politics are constituted (Whatmore 2006). Technology as articulation allows the recognition that humans are always in composition with nonhumanity, never outside of "a sticky web of connections or an ecology" (Bennett 2004, 365; see also Bennett 2009).

Digital assemblages are defined here as networks of humans, technologies, signs, and knowledges that constitute everyday life. There is no "outside" to such digital assemblages, and life as we know it is forever intertwined with digital technologies. Police investigations, then, are continually embedded in and are constituted by digital assemblages. This is to say, behaviors associated with sex crimes are ineluctably linked to technologies and knowledges in a way that both facilitates and hinders sex crime investigations. The internet and related digital communication technologies have enabled additional venues for sex crimes to take place. For example, child pornography can be distributed via the Dark Web,[1] and police investigators require specific software, knowledge, and skills to access such materials and track down engaged people. As they are often international in scope, such assemblages not only are difficult to investigate but also require a reorganization and redefinition of policing. North American police service organizations now have internet child exploitation units specifically dedicated to investigating digital sex crimes against children and the difficult task of finding offenders around the globe.

Concomitantly, sex crimes that are traditionally viewed as "offline," such as sexual assault, now generally have a digital component. Investigators increasingly use global positioning systems (GPS) not only to track down those accused of sex offenses but also to verify the whereabouts of both victims and offenders at the time of sexual assaults. Correspondences via e-mail and text between putative victim and offender, as we will show in chapter 3, become part of the investigations and part of the narrative to determine if an offense has been committed. Despite more of a digital trace, such investigations do not necessarily lead to more expedient and straightforward sex crime investigations. In addition, the toll, as we show in chapter 6 on police is increased and requires increasing amounts of emotional labor that were not required prior to the advent of the contemporary digital age.

DISCUSSION

In this chapter, we have outlined the legal background to investigating sex crimes across Canada, the United States, the United Kingdom, and Australia. We do so not only as a means of showing the similarities across English-speaking countries but also to note that, due to the nature of sex crimes, police officers tasked with investigating these crimes must negotiate with officers working across borders and jurisdictions. Nevertheless, the legal terrain that officers must know and navigate is complex and burdensome in terms of investigations. In addition, we offer the concept of digital assemblages as a means of understanding the digital technological infrastructure and knowledges, as well as practices, that are constitutive of investigation into sex crimes.

NOTE

1. The Dark Web is the World Wide Web content that exists on darknet: overlay networks that use the internet but require specific software, configurations, or authorization to access.

Chapter 3

"This Isn't Your Father's Police Force"

Digital Evidence in Sex Crime Investigations and the Need for Digital Policing

Digital information—including social media statuses, text and instant messages, and cell phone and security images or videos—increasingly serves as valuable evidence in sex crime cases (Carimico, Huynh, and Wells 2016; Diss 2013). For example, text, e-mail, and social media messages sent between the complainant and the accused before or after an alleged sexual assault, security camera footage demonstrating the intoxication level of a complainant before an alleged sexual assault, or even photographic or video documentation of the alleged assault transpiring each detail the context or content of criminal activity (Powell and Henry 2018; Bluett-Boyd et al. 2013; Powell 2010). In our digitized world, digital evidence, once considered as existing only in a small portion of criminal cases, frequently appears within all crime categories (Arnes 2018; Horsman 2017; Scanlan 2011; Yar 2013a, 2013b) and—according to the officers we interviewed—is an element in many (or arguably most) cases of sexual assault. Due to the especially difficult investigative process for sexual assault cases and the well-documented negative effects of these investigations on victims (Randall 2010; Jordan 2008), it is crucial to better understand the potentialities and pitfalls that digital evidence creates for sex crime investigations.

Due to the ubiquity of digital technology, our everyday practices and interactions now frequently leave a wake of digital information (e.g., text message conversations, GPS tracking, and internet search histories) (boyd, 2010), resulting in the infusion of digital evidence into many cases of sexual violence (Powell and Henry 2018). This generates a need for novel investigative tools for and approaches to police investigations. While the need to digitize the policing of primarily "cyber" sex crimes such as child pornography (as this crime has largely become a technology-facilitated activity) is widely accepted (Powell and Henry 2018; Scanlan 2011), much less scholarly and policy attention is focused on the role of digital evidence in the investigation of other sex crimes. The growing importance of digital evidence in sex crime cases shows the necessity of analyzing how police understand the potential capacity and pitfalls of gathering and utilizing digital evidence.

As Powell, Stratton, and Cameron assert in their theorization of digital criminology, digital technology has "had significant effects for everyday life and for everyday crimes" (2018, vi). While other advances in science and technology (e.g., DNA) have had substantial impacts on criminal investigations, digital technology's ubiquity has changed the very fabric of our lives and, thus, our crimes (Powell, Stratton, and Cameron 2018). While theories of cybercrime (Chaikin 2006; Clifford, 2006) have wrestled with the specific challenges for policing crimes committed online or using computer technology, we now recognize the need to assess digital technology's impacts on all sex crime categories and criminal investigations (Powell, Stratton, and Cameron 2018; Yar 2013a, 2013b).

Recognizing that any separation between "cyber" and "offline" investigations propagates the false dichotomy between our "online" and "offline" lives and crimes (Baym 2011; Powell, Stratton, and Cameron 2018), in this chapter we demonstrate how digital evidence is embedded in digital assemblages and affects the policing of sex crimes (and policing more broadly). We examine the changing nature of evidence in the digital era and police officers' interpretations of these changes. Showing how the opportunities and challenges of digital evidence are understood in the context of policing sex crimes, in this chapter we examine several challenges digital evidence brings to investigative processes and how it changes the resources and skills required by police officers and organizations. In relation to sex crimes, we show that all officers have not yet accepted the digital shift in investigations and that this shift has not been sufficiently accounted for in terms of resources, skills, and knowledge development within policing organizations.

We demonstrate that police officers feel they need more tools and training to effectively respond to the role that digital evidence increasingly plays in sex crimes. Following the maxim "this isn't your father's police force anymore" provided by one of our participants, we demonstrate that the substantial societal changes brought on by the digital age have had particular effects on the nature of sex crime investigations, and such effects need to be better understood and integrated into policing and the criminal justice system more broadly.

We divide the current chapter into two sections. In the first section, we review the literature on the changing nature of evidence and policing in the digital age. In the second section, we analyze and discuss police perspectives on how the proliferation of digital evidence is changing sex crime investigative practices and modifying the skills and resources needed within sex crime units. We show that, as sex crimes become increasingly digitized, it is necessary for sex crime policing to become digitized as well.

DIGITAL EVIDENCE AND THE NEED FOR DIGITAL POLICING

The upsurge in digital evidence in police investigations arises from the increase and rapid change in technological advances, and in the use and access to technologies (such as the internet and smartphones) that have, regardless of age, led to the erasure between online and offline in the everyday lives of most people on the planet (Powell, Stratton, and Cameron 2018). The extent to which we utilize technology to communicate and develop social networks (Baym 2011) increases the probability that a crime will involve some amount of digital evidence. Just as digital evidence has had a considerable impact on the practice of law (Gottehrer 2015; Kerr 2005), digital evidence has also provided many new opportunities and challenges for police practices and investigations (BBC News 2016; Brown 2015; Yar 2012, 2013b). Exemplifying the impact of digital evidence, participants at the 2014 Police Executive Research Forum discussed the importance of digital evidence for policing, with one attendee stating that digital evidence is now "as important as firearms, fingerprints, DNA" and that "more cases are being solved on digital evidence than anything else right now" (Goodison, Davis, and Jackson 2015, 14).

Digital evidence[1] differs from tangible evidence in that it includes "any digital data that contains reliable information that can support or refute a hypothesis of an incident of crime" (Arnes 2018, 7; Casey 2011; Gottehrer 2015). This data is not only collected from computers but also obtained through the examination of various digital devices such as smartphones, GPS systems, and digital cameras and video cameras (Arnes 2018; DeGaine 2013; Chaikin 2006). Each device can provide digital information—such as e-mail and text histories, internet search histories, GPS tracked movements, and digital images—that can be used to support or refute the validity of a claim (Casey 2011). Digital evidence, therefore, offers more opportunities for uncovering evidence (e.g., it is more common to find a "snapshot" of a criminal act in progress) yet also new challenges (e.g., missing context beyond the recorded image) for policing and the criminal justice system more broadly (Gottehrer 2015; Kerr 2005).

The affordances of digital technology—such as the ability to record, copy, distribute, and archive data quickly and easily—along with its omnipresence have resulted in our everyday interactions leaving extensive digital traces (boyd 2010). Not only are there many sources for digital evidence, but such devices have the capacity to produce and store massive amounts of data (Losavio, Seigfried-Spellar, and Sloan 2016). Although potentially very useful, digital evidence requires knowledge and skills to identify, collect, analyze, and store data from a plethora of digital sources in order to ensure that the evidence is useful in charging and prosecuting offenders. Digital forensics assist in validating the specific challenges concerning the authentication of digital data (Giordano 2004). In relation to sex crimes, such authentication can be at diverse scales, from the collection of text messages between two adults in a local sexual assault case to the global transmission of child pornography on the so-called Dark Web.

While digital evidence refers to sources of data, digital forensics addresses the systematic and scientific methods for the collection and preservation of data (Palmer 2001), which increases the validity of data and preserves the integrity of evidence in police investigations (Irons and Lallie 2014; Tun et al. 2016). This is important because the evidentiary principles of the courts place certain limitations on what sorts of digital evidence can be submitted and accepted into proceedings, which has "hyper-formalized" digital evidence and analysis (Beebe 2009, 21). Moreover, digital forensics techniques are increasingly applied at the beginning of investigations (rather than after, like in the past) to reduce the potential that evidence will be compromised (see Beebe 2009). Notwithstanding the positive impact of these procedures, debates exist concerning the validation of digital forensics due to its "interdisciplinary" nature (Losavio, Seigfried-Spellar, and Sloan 2016, 3). Without the full support of police organizations, the capacity of digital evidence to improve investigations and help solve crimes cannot be fully realized. For example, in relation to sex crimes, investigators may have to triage cases according to perceived threat and severity of the sexual violence, thereby leaving police unable to adequately respond to all cases in a timely manner.

Police officers, as the first responders and collectors of evidence (Lingwood, Smith, and Bond 2015), play a crucial role in the integration and impact of digital evidence in investigations. Policing practices have no doubt evolved over the years to adapt to various technological advancements. For example, the policing profession changed in response to the introduction of DNA comparison tests and biometrics (Faith and Bekir 2015). Both of these forms of scientific evidence have shown utility for identifying and excluding individuals during an investigation and have also required police to—sometimes radically—change their approach to investigations (Faith and Bekir 2015; Cole and Lynch 2006). While CCTV, desktop computers, and other technologies have constituted forms of electronic/digital evidence over the past several decades, the more recent proliferation of online technology and the rise of Web 2.0 (Yar 2012) require police to revisit their responses and practices and to manage the increasing ubiquity of digital evidence. Indeed, the prevalence of digital technology (including the proliferation of social media use and text messaging) dramatically recalibrates the skills police require during investigations. For example, as demonstrated by our research detailed in the section that follows, police in sex crime units are now regularly required to have the know-how to access a variety of social media sites and mobile applications to find and correctly document evidence of messages or images shared between victims and offenders. Notwithstanding the improvements that digital evidence can bring to the investigation stage, there are several challenges that digital evidence creates for policing practices.

Although digital evidence surely offers more information in many sexual assault cases, thus affording possible avenues for documenting these notoriously difficult-to-prove crimes, the quantity of digital information also creates new challenges for investigators who may not have the resources to sift through these "electronic haystacks" (Chaikin 2006), specifically, when police agencies do not have the training or resources necessary to access, analyze, and store digital data in a timely manner (Chaikin 2006; Irons and Lallie 2014). Gathering and analyzing digital data can be extremely time and resource intensive, requiring forensic tools and methods to ensure the verifiability of the evidence (Arnes 2018). Moreover, the potential use of digital evidence, for example, can be impacted by the lack of cooperation from social media sites to provide data (see Tun et al. 2016).

Another distinct but related challenge is the amount of organizational and officer acceptance and commitment to overcoming these challenges and the acceptance of digital evidence–related practices. In addition to resource shortcomings, cultural shortcomings exist due to what some perceive as a resistance to digital evidence by "old-timers who are not technical" and who are not accepting the pivotal role that digital evidence now plays for "policing in the 21st century" (Goodison, Davis, and Jackson 2015, 15). The scant research in the area of digital evidence, policing, and sex crimes demonstrates that police departments are struggling to handle the ever-increasing pool of digital information and to adjust to the rapid changes that such evidence engenders in their profession and professional practice (Powell and Henry 2018).

The retrieval, verification, and translation of information from digital devices can be costly, and police budgets are not increasing to accommodate for these costs or to adequately account for officer training in this area and the increased time lines for investigating cases involving digital evidence (see Gogolin 2010). Challenges to dealing with digital evidence include complicated and time-consuming training (e.g., digital forensics) that translates into inadequately trained officers, understaffed digital forensics units, lack of up-to-date equipment and/or dedicated digital forensics or cybercrime units in some areas, and the need to work with various third parties to access evidence (e.g., social media companies and internet/cell phone providers) (Goodison, Davis, and Jackson 2015; Powell and Henry 2018; Irons and Lallie 2014). The techniques required for policing in the digital age create the need for more immediate and regular training and knowledge of the implications of the digital world for responding to and investigating sexual violence (see Gogolin 2010). Specifically, police face the challenge of probing complex digital assemblages that have their own peculiarities that require knowledge not only of the sex crime being committed but also skills required to navigate networks of humans and technologies. They must know the meanings of signs within specific digital worlds; specifically, police investigators must know the terms and codes indigenous to platforms where sex crimes take place. As such, and in light of the ubiquity of digital evidence in sex crime cases demonstrated in the following section, it is necessary to understand how police perceive the challenge and opportunities of digital evidence in these cases.

POLICE PERSPECTIVES ON THE
IMPACT OF DIGITAL EVIDENCE

In the sections that follow, we discuss the key emergent themes among police perceptions of the role of and challenges tied to digital evidence in the policing of sex crimes. Officers express that the ubiquity of digital evidence in sex crime cases (since victims and offenders in sex crime cases almost always have a preexisting relationship that is somehow digitally documented) has led to manifold novel challenges such as backlogs created by a lack of staff to process large amounts of digital evidence (in already overburdened sex crime units); struggles to learn and keep up with rapid technological change (e.g., applicable technologies and online platforms); and investigator and organizational resistance to the increasing role of digital technology in cases of sexual assault (wherein technological know-how has not traditionally been understood as a necessary investigative skill). These obstacles led to assertions that digital evidence is a "double-edged sword" that not only provides more evidence to help solve (notoriously difficult to prove) sex crime cases (Randall 2010) but also generates new challenges that make these cases considerably more complex and may intensify the burden on both officers in sex crime investigative units and the victims of these crimes. Overall, sex crime investigator responses show a need for new or modified forms of policing that respond to the influx of digital evidence and organizationally acknowledge the digital shift in policing practices. Digital policing requires knowledge and skills to navigate the signs, languages, technologies, and manifold social media platforms comprising digital assemblages and the sex crimes that transpire vis-à-vis various digital assemblages.

"This Is the Age of Technology": The Ubiquity of Digital Evidence in Sex Crime Cases

Interviewee responses clearly demonstrate the need for more recognition and attention directed to the growing role played by digital evidence in sex crime cases. Sex crime investigators express that digital evidence is now an element in the vast majority of sex crime cases:

> **Brian:** [There is always digital evidence involved in a sex crime case] unless it's a true—which are rare—stranger-on-stranger [sexual assault], walking through the parking lot to your car at 10 o'clock and some stranger abducts her or, you know, they don't have a prior relationship at all. *This is the age of technology.* So most often our sex assaults and domestic violence—there's [digital] communication there, [. . .] there is some kind of relationship there. And if you're a teenager or even in your 20s, 30s, or 40s, you have a cell phone, and you have a computer, and there's some kind of dialogue and communication there. [. . .] [A]lmost all the time there's a phone involved in what I'm investigating. Or a computer—a phone or a computer.

> **Bradley:** I'd say the vast majority [of sex crimes] have some sort of technological component whether it's Facebook, whether it's texting, whether it's [. . .] social media. Because most sexual assaults are, [the] suspect is known to the victim. So there's a communication factor in there. [. . .] So given the fact that they know each other . . . if it's a co-worker, you're going to have in-office communication, there may be threats by e-mails. I don't know if I can give you a certain percentage, but I would say most investigations we do have some type of technological component to it. You know, whether it's harassment threats, texting, and stuff like that. That's just the way it falls because of the relationship factor.

These officers' comments highlight that, because most sex crime offenders are known to the victims, digital communication between the parties exists in almost all cases of sexual violence. The digital traces left by these digital conversations (via text message, social media messages, or e-mail) often become pieces of digital evidence that must be disentangled in terms of what was intended by the messages versus how each is interpreted within the processes of case construction. Echoing these sentiments, other investigators identify the extensive and complex role that social media and texting archives now play in the investigation of sexual assaults. Officers explain that victims and offenders may "communicate with each other before, after, or during an offence" (Samantha), meaning that in most cases "somehow technology [is] involved in the investigation" (Brenda). Officers put forth that digital evidence tends to only be lacking in the rare case of a sexual assault wherein the victim and offender are strangers. As the following officer expresses, the search for digital evidence is now often their first step in a case:

> **Darryl:** When somebody comes in with an investigation, depending on what type it is, I mean first thing you do is to ask someone consent if we can take your phone because we're looking for communication between the suspect and the victim, any type of communication.

Responses like Darryl's demonstrate that there has been a considerable shift in the policing of sex crimes due to technological innovations and ubiquity. Such a dramatic shift in technology mediates relationships that constitute sex crimes and elaborates the complexity of police response to these crimes (Manning 2008). From the beginning of an investigation, the digital component of a case figures prominently. As shown in both Bradley's and Darryl's responses, police must determine the level of communication between the offender and victim *and* interpret the nature and intention of the communications. This added layer of investigation impacts both the labor process (e.g., how sex crimes are approached) and workload (e.g., time required to process and interpret evidence when constructing the theory of the crime) of officers in particularly dramatic ways in sex crime units.

Increasing Levels of Digital Evidence, Insufficient Resources, and the Backlog Problem

The changes in sex crime investigations brought on by digital technologies often increase the volume of evidence that needs to be cataloged and sorted. In the majority of police services included in our study, this has led to backlogs and considerable wait times as understaffed—or nonexistent—tech units force their few trained officers to be overburdened with the task of accessing, storing, and analyzing a large number of digital devices and online accounts. As the following officer explains, in her unit they are forced to rely on the technological know-how of their one-member internet child exploitation (ICE) unit to help with technology-related evidence for the entire sex crime unit:

Serena: [In addition to the ICE officer's own child exploitation cases], what would also happen is he would also get all the phones, all the computers, he would get everything. So he is so bombarded, it is impossible to get anything done [. . .] with the sheer volume of stuff that comes in.

Serena describes how the police department in her area has not provided enough staff and organizational support to keep up with the huge influx in digital evidence. Depending on their location, officers expressed this sentiment to varying degrees, as some areas were seen to have understaffed digital forensic units while others had no dedicated unit or one investigator to fulfill the digital forensic needs of the entire police service organization.

Despite most officers acknowledging that digital technology and digital know-how are now integral parts of sex crime policing, many express that the organizational structure of sex crime units has not adequately changed to reflect and support the new role of digital technology in these cases. This was demonstrated, for example, in the reported dearth of hiring for technologically skilled staff:

Brenda: We're completely understaffed when it comes to our tech crimes people so those people who are supposed to be assisting us to glean that information [about digital components of sex crime cases] we have very few people that [. . .] actually do that work for us.

Marissa: The impact of digital evidence on sex crimes increases the need for digital forensic units and officers at all levels that understand digital technology and various social media platforms. [. . .] The amount of cases we get now involving the technology, the cyber stuff, has increased exponentially. And we have not been equipped at the same pace.

The huge increase in the volume of digital evidence in sex crime cases has not been met with an equal increase in resources and staffing for digital forensic units and training to allow all officers to deal with this evidence to some extent. Officers describe how the organizational structures of police units have not changed enough to accommodate the percentage of cases that require the ability to navigate digital assemblages, in terms of knowledges of digital forensics and technological skills. Many police services are relying on understaffed tech crime and digital forensic units—or as noted, a single tech-savvy officer. Officers describe relying on the cohort of younger officers who—due to growing up with digital technology—tend to have more digital know-how:

Edward: Oh [the digital component] has been huge. [. . .] It has made greater demands on us, investigatively. And kind of presuming we have a knowledge that we might not have. [. . .] The new hires who are under 35 have a lot of familiarity with social media, some people have very little—but there is the presumption that you can deal with it and that you'll be competent.

Anthony: I learn from partners, and all the new guys who are coming up are so much more technical savvy, techno-savvy, you have to learn from them to carry on because that's more of our job now.

Shirley: As far as technology goes, it really depends. You can get somebody who's been on the road for a couple of years. They're 22 or 23 years old. They know Facebook, they know Kik, they know what all those applications are. They can get basic information and it's very easy [for them]. And somebody else, who has 35 years of service, they're calling and they're on "the Facebooks" [. . .]. You know what I mean? But yeah as far as training goes, I think we can definitely improve as far as providing investigative skills to members up front, as far as best practices in terms of how to handle exhibits [of evidence].

These officers describe relying on the technological know-how that younger officers *happen* to have. Thus, the ability of a given sex crime unit to effectively investigate crimes with a digital evidence element may be arbitrarily related to the abilities officers happen to possess. Such practices do not result in the production of a community of practice (Wenger 2000) but, rather, the exchange of knowledge and practice on an ad hoc basis.

Recognizing that increasing levels of digital evidence in sex crime cases have not been met with adequate human and material supports, many officers report attempting "to train themselves" to deal with this evidence, particularly that tied to social media sites. As training cannot be readily established for every new technological application and would become obsolete in a matter of months, officers who are more equipped to teach themselves or learn informally from other officers are identified as best able to keep up with the digital turn in policing. Many asserted that they would like to have more training on how to find and properly handle digital evidence. Some mentioned requesting technology-related investigative courses, and others who had received training on internet evidence analysis, cell phone forensics, and network investigative techniques mentioned that the training needed to be completed more frequently to keep up with constantly changing technology. Officers also mentioned, however, that often overburdened sex crime units do not have enough officers to allow for frequent absences for training. Yet it may be necessary to prioritize this training, as many officers assert that the *most difficult* part of modern sex crime investigations is keeping up with the rapid rate of technological change.

Resistance to Digital Policing

Many officers expressed that organizational shortcomings are aggravated by a portion of supervisors and officers who, they feel, are resistant to the focus on digital evidence in current sex crime investigations. In essence, officers felt that some colleagues opted to not fully recognize the necessary shift toward digital policing that must occur in sex crime units:

> **Steven:** Some of the higher-ups and old boys [. . .] haven't been on the road in many years and I don't think they understand the complexities of investigations now. Like if you investigated an assault 10–15 years ago, you're not talking about three production orders to get the Rogers[2] information and to get the search warrant for the property locker and the phone, and getting the production order for the app[lication] that they've used on the phone—like, you didn't have all that stuff a couple years ago. You would write your simple search warrant to get into a house to get the knife. The technology has made our investigations lengthier and more complex and more time consuming and not everyone understands that, I don't think, at this point.

> **Matthew:** Everybody uses Facebook nowadays, and [it's an issue for those who] don't know how to get to Facebook or capture the information that's on Facebook—just with a screen capture, whatever it takes. But that's the challenge because we're dealing with an older [police] regime. In most police services you've got the old guys that say "I used to solve crimes on pen and paper, I don't need the computer, because we did a great job back then"—but it's a completely different world. This isn't your father's police force anymore, and that's one of the big challenges we have is the resources in our office and within the service—people just don't have the tech backgrounds yet. Now as we hire younger guys they come with that because they know nothing else but tech. So, that's helping a bit but we're still severely backlogged.

These cases of individual resistance to new technology's role in policing sex crimes, as these officers describe, may further stall attempts to acquire adequate supports and resources for digital-era investigations. While "cops typically aren't, you know, tech savvy, computer people" (Christie), our research findings show that there remains ample evidence that more "tech-savvy" officers are required to optimize policing processes and meet investigative needs. Said another way, while sex crime policing now regularly demands digital policing, many officers are not as digitally literate as these units now call for. Thus, there is need for a system-wide recognition across all ranks of officers that more technologically informed and trained officers are required if sex crime units are going to keep up with the technological advancements that broadly impact the nature of investigations in this area.

The increase in digital evidence—and its impact on the investigation process—has changed the nature of sex crime policing in substantial ways. The traditional organizational structures are no longer adequate as, for instance, a sex crime investigator may now need to be in close proximity to the ICE unit as many officers now rely on the expertise of ICE unit members when working the technological aspects of physical sexual assaults: "I liaise all the time with ICE guys [. . .] and I'm always in that office back and forth because we're working pretty [closely], we're separated but we're intertwined" (William). Thus, officers described the structure of policing units as inadequate for facilitating the necessary cooperation between units with diverse specializations (e.g., sexual violence versus cybercrime and technology) as demanded by the changing nature of sexual violence investigations. Whereas technological supports differ considerably depending on the specific police organization, with a few officers saying they felt they were well supported by their present tech provisions, the norm across agencies remained a backlog in overburdened tech units and a lack of training. Thus, police organizations will need to create awareness about how the digital shift in sex crime policing challenges the typical demarcation of certain units, introduce regular technology training, and hire personnel dedicated to processing electronic evidence and assisting in technological aspects of investigations. This process of boundary spanning (Giacomantonio 2014; Aldrich and Herker 1977) requires an initial recognition that sex crimes take place within a digitized world and that the organization's internal networks and orientation must adapt to this external reality (see Manning 2008). Such a move would increase the absorptive capacity (Zahra and George 2002) of the organization to technological changes that invariably have implications for sexual assault cases.

Digital Evidence as a Double-Edged Sword

Digital evidence was seen by officers as a double-edged sword: digital evidence affords more convincing evidence in some cases but also makes cases much lengthier and more invasive for victims of sex crimes. In terms of the former, officers described how having more evidence available—namely, in cases that would have traditionally been a case of "he-said she-said"—provides more context around each situation:

Brian: There's been a real shift. When I started in 1991, you didn't have the text messages. You didn't have the social media [. . .] evidence that you get now. [. . .] I think, especially the cases where you have usually there's only two people there [. . .]—the victim and the accused—and you have one word against the other, [. . .] it certainly helps the case if we can back it up with some text messages. One way or the other, whether it's for or against the accused, to me as an investigator it's an advantage to have those.

Lewis: I can tell you that numerous times sitting with a victim and they pull out their phone—well look, he texted me this, or he said this, or she said this, and it's all there. Way back when we didn't have that and it was mostly just—well he called me or he said this. We used to tell people like, for instance in a harassment case, every time you get a call, write it down. The date, time, what he said—well now it's all here and time stamped. So that's changed things.

Lois: [Before 2007] most of our files were he-said she-said, and then once social media evolved almost every file that we had—or a lot of them—had to do with social media, and [. . .] in a lot of ways it provided you with some really great evidence. Although the investigation was prolonged [by the warrant process], it provided, ya know for instance, a teenager involved in a relationship with an older male, and obviously because of their age they couldn't consent, and they were texting or sexting or whatever or talking about the sexual experience they had, you put those text messages in front of the guy, ya know, what can he say and then you end up getting a bit of a slam dunk confession which makes for this teenager not to have to testify really at the end of the day.

As shown here, digital technologies not only liberate investigators from having to prove communications between victim and offender but also serve as a mode of verification to claims of sexual assault (a crime that has been long regarded as particularly difficult to investigate and prove) (cf. Jewkes 2013; Powell and Henry 2018; Wall 2007; Wall and Williams 2007). As Brian noted in his interview, digitally recorded communication has shifted the manner in which sex crime investigations are carried out. These digital conversation archives provide previously unavailable evidence that can help interpret the accuracy of the, often conflicting, perspectives of the complainant and accused. Digital evidence, an officer explained, can act as "digital breadcrumbs" (Brianna) that lead to the offender. In some cases, it challenges the "he-said she-said" (Powell 2010) nature of sexual violence cases and provides evidence that lessens the well-documented burden of testimony for sex crime victims (Randall 2010). Reflecting on Lewis's words, we see that the time line afforded through texting can provide officers the evidence necessary to lay a charge and relieve the victim from having to document some instances of harassment by hand. Lois evinces that, in instances of text messages between a minor and an adult, this sort of evidence can elicit a confession and reduce the stress on witness testimony. In such cases, digital evidence is perceived to act as the perfect "digital witness."

Despite the utility of "digital breadcrumbs" in sex crime investigations, the other side of the sword's edge is that digital evidence—though seemingly delivering a neutral account—may not provide the full story and that the management of digital evidence can be extremely time consuming for officers and invasive for victims. Early research shows that officers need to be careful to interpret this evidence in the context of the online world and to understand that interpretations of digital evidence (especially in cases of sexual violence) are malleable despite their "neutral" appearance (Powell 2015; Slane 2015). For example, as complainants' post-assault social media and text conversations become a common form of evidence in sexual assault trials, scholars are recognizing how this evidence can be misused against the complainant due to misconceptions about how a victim should act following a sexual assault based on stereotypes of sexual assault victims and victimization (Bluett-Boyd et al. 2013; Powell 2015). Some officers described how, through a reliance on these same stereotypes about sexual violence, social media evidence might be used against complainants in the court process, and, thereby, this evidence may actually make the case more difficult to prove at times. For instance, the following officer's statements show the reliance on digital evidence may be misguided in some cases:

> **James:** [The defense looks at the victim's social media account and says] "Oh look, she went to a party and she's gloating about how she kissed this guy. Yet it's sexual assault." You know, like I'm a [social media] creeper. And I will always bring up social media to my victim if, especially if I find stuff that basically contradicts what they're saying. Because I find that it's harder to prove in court, especially when I know that [the] defense is gonna use that. And they do it a lot. Like I lost a case because of it. Where a sexual assault, it was legit. It happened. But yet, because she was seen on social media, and there's pictures of her with the accused, laughing and having drinks after the fact. She couldn't tell us when those pictures happened. So, we lost the case because the judge didn't believe that she purposefully stayed away from him after. Do you know what I mean? "If you're that scared, why're you still hanging out with him?" kind of thing.

James feels that digital evidence worked counter to proving the truth of the case. In this case, social media evidence was used to argue that the victim was not acting "as a victim should" following a sexual assault, and thus the defendant was not found guilty. In this case, the digital "trace" that is offered does not provide an objective account of the truth but is, like all evidence, open to (mis)interpretation and can count against sexual assault victims.

Officers also expressed high levels of frustration with how much longer it takes to investigate sex crimes that include digital evidence and how this makes their jobs more difficult and negatively impacts victims. Even for those investigators with digital technology know-how and adequate training, digital evidence has provided many new challenges related to cross-jurisdictional cases and data requests that significantly slow down investigations. For instance, one officer discussed how something as simple as needing to see a conversation between an accused and complainant that occurred on Kik[3] can slow down an investigation as there is a lengthy wait time to get a warrant to receive the information and to get access granted from the company, followed by an additional wait time for the forensic examiner to review the device. Max further explains that digital evidence, by slowing down cases, creates frustrating wait times for victims:

> **Max:** So, when people say why is this investigation taking so long, well we're waiting to get the evidence in order to get the reasonable probable grounds to lay the charge. So there's a lot as far as the technology side with just phones and computers right? There's a lot. And even with Facebook messages and having to write a MLAT, which is an international type warrant for a company outside of Canada, that's [. . .] a lot. So any sexual assault investigation or any investigation involving social media and stuff can be time consuming.

Officers, as evidenced in Max's account, were frustrated about the amount of time and effort necessary to get a warrant or production order to access digital information from companies such as Facebook that are located outside of Canada. Officers are now required to do long international warrant processes for a huge portion of cases. Where once this kind of cross-jurisdictional, complex case was rare, it is seemingly becoming the norm in sex crime policing. Officers discuss how search warrants that used to be two sentences long to access someone's home now take multiple days to fill out in order to access something like an IP address. A lack of cooperation or timeliness from internet service providers (ISPs) or social media corporations can also create difficult hurdles for police to manage (Powell and Henry, 2018). Thus, due to a combination of the backlogs in many digital forensic units and the time required to acquire complex warrants for digital evidence, officers express concern for the increased wait times victims experienced, which can have impacts, including victims opting to no longer pursue the case, remembering less detail at trial, or being revictimized by reliving the case details after a prolonged period. These concerns are especially noteworthy given the notoriously high level of sex crime victims who report being revictimized or otherwise dissatisfied with the reporting and investigation process (Randall 2010; Jordan 2008).

Officers also expressed that victims—especially teenagers—are very upset when they have to give up their phones for long periods of time. This is especially acute when they are going through a challenging time in their life as a result of sexual victimization. As one officer expressed, the phone is often their lifeline to connect to friends and family, and to have a phone taken away for multiple weeks or months can be extremely difficult. According to

Edward, it can also feel like the police are taking away "their safety." Some officers even said that they've had teenager complainants who would rather not continue with a case if it requires giving up their phone for a long time:

> **Sarah:** Yeah, we've taken some steps here to try to get through the phones very quickly, but [especially for teenagers] it is literally like they're giving you their arm. [. . .] [W]e're glad they came forward, [. . .] we don't want to give them any reasons not to come forward in the future if something happens again. And simply keeping holding on to their cell phone for a long time to a kid could be something that really would prevent them from coming forward again.

> **Henry:** Both here and our RCMP labs are so backlogged with victims' phones we can call the tech-crime lab and say look can I get a quicker turn-around, so I can get back this victim's phone. You don't want to leave them without their phone, they have already been victimized enough. They will try to push them up the queue, but at the end of the day, you got a homicide going on, ya got an active, ya know—it is what it is. They are so backlogged that it makes it difficult ya know. There is a huge backlog in tech-crime.

These comments on the long wait times and need to take victims' phones demonstrate that digital evidence may be amplifying the already extremely difficult experience of being a victim of sexual violence in the criminal justice system. Therefore, while in some cases digital information may provide "game-changing" (Powell 2015) evidence in a case that would otherwise have floundered in court, digital evidence has also had negative side effects such as slowing down police investigations and allowing for more intrusive investigations of complainant behavior. This mix of very negative and very positive effects expressed by police demonstrates the double-edged sword of digital evidence and the variety of challenges and opportunities for policing in the digital age.

DISCUSSION

Here, in chapter 3, we demonstrate that the separation between "cyber" and "offline" investigations is now a false dichotomy in sex crime cases, as "traditional" sex crimes now regularly include digital evidence and require digital policing. Whereas the nature of investigating sex crimes in the digital era has undergone a significant shift, we show that not all officers accept this shift and that it has not been adequately accounted for within policing organizations in terms of resources, skill, and knowledge development. Specifically, our analysis demonstrates how digital evidence taxes the resources of sex crime units and challenges their capacity to address the knowledge and time demands of collecting, processing, and cataloging digital evidence. Based on these findings, a revamping of education or skill requirements for police that extend beyond traditional police foundations and police college curriculum to include computer science, computer programming, forensic sciences, and other such diploma-or degree-based programs may be value-added considerations for police organizations as technology becomes increasingly salient in societal living (and thus criminal acts).

Although concerns may vary somewhat depending on the police organization or unit we interviewed, the difficulties police face are a derivative of the increasingly digital world. Yar (2013a) notes that traditional agencies of criminal justice are largely underequipped and poorly adapting to the realities of policing in the digital age. Shortages in technologically trained personnel mean that investigations take longer to complete and require more resources to do so. In sex crime cases specifically, the infusion of digital evidence has presented as a double-edged sword that provides both more evidence and new challenges for police and victims. While officers express that digital evidence may provide more conclusive proof in the notoriously difficult pursuit of proving sexual assault charges, they are also concerned that this evidence may be unfairly used against victims at trial and may make cases lengthier and more invasive for victims.

NOTES

1. In this chapter, we focus on evidence; however, it is important to note the difference between intelligence and evidence. Evidence is "the available body of facts or information indicating whether a belief or proposition is true or valid and intelligence is: the ability to acquire and apply knowledge and skills or the collection of information of military or political value" (Irons and Lallie 2014, 589).

2. A Canadian telecommunications company.

3. Kik Messenger, commonly called Kik, is a freeware instant messaging mobile application from Kik Interactive.

Chapter 4

"Society Wants to See a True Victim"

Police Interpretations of Victims of Sexual Violence

In Canada, dedicated feminist activism has resulted in various changes to sexual assault legislation aimed at undermining myths about sexual violence (e.g., the myth that you cannot sexually assault your spouse) and addressing the revictimization of victims of sexual violence within the criminal justice system. For instance, Criminal Code of Canada amendments passed in 1983 reformed the law that excluded spouses from being charged with sexual assault (Randall 2010), and in 1997, limits were placed on defense lawyers' access to victims' personal records (Sheehy 2012). These legislative changes were intended to reduce the emphasis on victim behavior (e.g., no longer discrediting the victim based on their past sexual activities) and increase the focus on the violence committed by the perpetrator (Sheehy 2012; Randall 2010). The 1983 reforms saw the rise in the rate of sexual offenses reported to police, which continued steadily until 1993 until it peaked at 135 incidents per one hundred thousand population. Since 1993, there was a steady decline, resulting in a 1997 rate that was 25 percent lower than the peak of 1993. Although such legislative change can be understood as representing a partial movement away from victim blaming, there remain many complexities in the policing of sexual victimization, including within the context of navigating evidence and consent.

Evidencing the continued shortcomings of police responses to victims of sexual violence, a 2017 report found that one in five sexual assault claims are dismissed as baseless by Canadian police (Doolittle 2017). Perhaps not surprising, in 2017, the Trudeau government called a national inquiry into cases of sexual victimization deemed unfounded. The existence of an inquiry alone suggests that legislation and practice, despite ongoing efforts, may inadvertently keep victims of sexual violence in a subordinate position, disempowered, and voiceless. In addition, officers are torn as they struggle to represent the voiceless and disempowered and, simultaneously, to protect those who are falsely accused from the sex offender stigma and grapple with deeply embedded myths about sexual violence and sexual violence victims (Ricciardelli and Moir 2013; Ricciardelli and Spencer 2017).

Recognizing the lack of empirical knowledge on police that respond to and investigate sexual violence, in this chapter we draw on interviews with officers working in internet child exploitation (ICE), sex crime, and child abuse units to understand how police interpret and respond to child, youth, and adult victims of sex crimes. Specifically, we examine the seeming range of police interpretation of victims, from those whose victimization is perceived as obvious (e.g., undoubtedly a victim of a sex crime) to those whose victimization is perceived as more challenging to support professionally (e.g., a victim whose claims cannot be substantiated with evidence that surpasses the standard of reasonable doubt). Next, we explore if and how interpretations of victims translate into police perceptions of their interactions with victims (e.g., how officers feel the victim can be treated) and their interpretations of the possible outcomes that can be offered in the investigation (e.g., charges laid). We highlight the difficulties officers encounter as they strive to balance their occupational role with victim needs, always paying heed to the fact that officer dispositions impact how victims judge the justice meted out in the wake of their victimization (Bradford, Jackson, and Stanko 2009; Wemmers 2010).

SEX CRIMES, POLICE, AND VICTIMS

In the policing of sex crimes, little is known about police interpretations of victims—an undeniably difficult concept to measure. Concerns arise as the percentage of sex crime cases considered "unfounded" remains higher than for other crimes and continues to vary widely between provinces in Canada, demonstrating that high rates are not solely due to the challenging nature of proving the act occurred (Benoit et al. 2015, 8; Light and Ruebsaat 2006). Researchers continue to assert that gender bias (Martin 2005) and rape myths (Spohn, Tellis, and O'Neal 2015) influence the way *some* (not all) police officers understand and respond to sexual violence (Jordan 2001). For example, Jan Jordan (2001) argues that police and sexual assault survivors remain "worlds apart" in their interpretations of sexual victimization, including in the needs of police versus victims in investigations and outcomes. One of the reasons behind this division, she argues, is that police rely on stereotypes and may expect victims to be "perfect" in terms of their behaviors and their ostensible culpability in their victimization (Jordan 2008). Jordan, in the context of any exchange preceding sexual contact between adults, suggests that such an exchange is nearly always debatable in its role as a presignaling of consent. Interpretations of consent—the idea that one may truly believe the pending sexual partner does consent—draws into question the intent to victimize by the accused, which complicates investigations and criminal processes (Randall 2010).

The notion of a perfect or an "ideal victim" then provides the interpretive framework for public and media interpretations of victims of sex crimes, with child victims receiving the greatest level of sympathy (Christie 1986; Davies, Francis, and Greer 2007; Dunn 2010). For Christie, an ideal victim "must be strong enough to be listened to, or dare to talk. But she (he [they]) must at the very same time be weak enough not to become a threat to other important interests" (1986, 21). In addition, victims must be seen as not, in any way, contributing to their victimization by not being in the "wrong" places at the "wrong" times with the "wrong" people. Legal requirements about evidence and demonstrating "beyond reasonable doubt" to secure convictions ensure these frameworks guide officers' interpretations of sex crime victims, at least in some capacity, given the reciprocal effect they place on their investigations and ability to respond to such offenses. To this end, Jordan (2001, 679) explains that "little in the way of substantive improvements appears possible within this historically and cross-cultural fraught area." Of course, despite what can be done (i.e., if charges can be laid or not), how police respond to victims of sex crimes is invaluable for ensuring that victims are "being treated fairly and with respect—[which] is as important as the outcome of the case" (Johnson 2015, 4). The need for a victim to feel heard and believed is fundamental but may not always be compatible with the law and arguably with the temperament of all officers working in sex crime units.

Scholars continuously underscore the role of police "culture" as determinative of police dispositions more broadly and toward child and adult sex crime victims specifically (Chan 1997; Crank 2014; Finkelhor, Wolak, and Berliner 2001; Prokos and Padavic 2002). Police culture is generally accepted to encompass the shared values and attitudes (Paoline, Meyers, and Worden 2000) that assist officers in dealing with the demands of their occupation (Crank 1998); however, it varies by detachment, is influenced by structural realities, and is not homogeneous (Spencer et al. 2019). As such, even with progressive reforms at the policy and training levels not all officers or policing units equally adopt these changes (Benoit et al. 2015; Light and Ruebsaat 2006). Van Maanen (1984), for instance, argues in his ethnographic study in a police training program that, although policing recruits enter the occupation motivated and committed, over time officer behavior fell in line with the detachment or organizational norms. Thus, despite official training and applied and onsite teaching, detachment norms or culture may have more influence on behaviors over time for officers. This policing in practice versus policing on the books phenomenon is similar to the shortcomings legal feminists have noted in terms of the lackluster changes seen in sexual assault trials despite the feminist-informed changes made to sexual assault legislation (Randall 2010; Smart 1989).

Overall, beyond the broad umbrella of offenses and processes that both define and are defined as sex crimes and thus ultimately guide police response, police sets of beliefs and ideals shape police practice and investigations into sex crimes. Together, both still only offer part of the context under which police interpret and respond to sex crimes. Researchers have concluded that legally relevant and irrelevant case characteristics influence police responses (Tasca et al., 2013), particularly in the case of sexual assault responses. Due to the variance of recognition of sex crime victims, analysts have continuously confirmed the politics of the label of victim both within broader society and within policing (Crenshaw 1991; Elias 1986; Walklate 2006; McGarry and Walklate 2015; Walklate et al. 2019). As an outcome of the politics of victimization, some individuals who experience events of victimization are accorded full status as victims, and others are rendered invisible. Such an outcome of invisibility is often predicated on deeper forms of marginalization-based categories of race, class, and gender that work to disadvantage victims as they report sexual assaults to police (Crenshaw 1991; Sokoloff and DuPont 2005).

These conceptualizations of victim status effectively guide broader public understandings of who is a victim and may impinge on criminal justice personnel's interpretations of events of victimization and the victims of whom they are tasked to respond. In this chapter, we examine how investigators reflect not only broader conceptions of sex crime victims but also traditional policing interpretations of child and adult victims of crime. We examine the dispositions that guide how police investigate and respond to victims of sex crimes as a means of providing insight into how and why sex crime victims may experience different treatment by police officers. We show that police adherence to or rejection of understandings of the "ideal victim" shapes their interpretations of sexual violence and sexual violence victims. In addition, we reveal that such understandings are shaped by structural and cultural influences that define police responses—which slowly evolve with growing awareness and activism.

POLICE INTERPRETATIONS OF SEX CRIMES

We structure the results to frame how police understand and respond to sex crime victims who are either perceived as "ideal"—without a doubt a person who has been the victim of a sex crime that can be substantiated beyond reasonable doubt—or not ideal. The latter refers to a victim whose claims are perceived as not feasible, legally "unfounded" or "unfound-able," given the scope of the police officers' occupational parameters. We present how police translate victim "status" and how they see this status as impacting their investigative approaches and outcomes (i.e., determining if charges can or cannot be laid). Finally, we present the reflexive dispositions toward victims that some investigators engage, including rebuffing the use of stereotypes and victim blaming in engaging with sexual assault victims and the difficulties they encounter as they strive to balance their occupational role with victim needs.

The ideal victim is a person or category of individuals who, when victimized, are most readily attributed the complete and legitimate status of being a victim (Christie 1986). The legitimate status of the victim is contingent upon, among other things, the social, cultural, and economic background of the victim as well as the legal circumstances surrounding their experience of victimization. As such, the concept of the ideal victim points to the intersectional components of how some individuals in society—for instance, adult women and racialized populations who experience structural inequalities (Bowleg 2012)—are denied victim status. To be an ideal victim, in a legal sense, requires there to be either physical evidence to support the described event and/or no doubt that the sexual acts were nonconsensual. Given that some populations cannot consent to sexual acts, the concept of the ideal victim points to how the label of victim is automatically awarded to certain individuals.

Child victims, particularly, are accorded status as "real" victims. Although the category of child is a relatively recent convention (Aries 1965, 2012), childhood refers to a particular stage of life rather than a group of individuals implied by the term "children" (Heywood 2001). Within this framework, children are simultaneously viewed as the future and as innocent, unable to understand the full consequences of their actions and unable to freely consent or be distrusting when approached by an adult who holds a position of authority (Kraftl 2008). Many of the police officers in our study offered this perspective:

Bill: Because these [child victims of sexual abuse] are the truest victims. This— there is nowhere else. I mean, it's funny, I razz my counterparts in homicide, and say "well you know, if you want to deal with a real victim, you come and see me." Not saying they're not true victims in the homicide world, but often you hear in the media [about] gang related, things like that. But these [children] are victims that can't protect themselves. So that's what we have to do.

Michael: [T]he people here are real victims. And I don't mean to diminish anyone else's victimization; however, most people have made a decision or series of decisions that results in them being in a situation where they find themselves being victimized. Whereas opposed to kids that are subject to the decisions of others to victimize them. And even where they are making decisions, they are uninformed decisions because of their age, maturity, lack of sophistication, so you have true victims, right? Who are victims of the circumstances they have found themselves in, as opposed to have created themselves.

In the first quote, Bill frames the child as a person in need of protection, thus innocent and prey to victimization if anyone was to assert their power. In relation to Officer Bill's response, we see that his disposition toward child victims places him at odds with other police units within his police organization—he perceives his victims as ideal, undeniable victims in comparison to any adult victim where he believes there can be more ambiguity around the facts of the criminality. His view is that child victims are the truest victims, comparing them to adult homicide victims, because, for instance, a child's lifestyle is at the discretion of their caretakers and other such factors beyond their control that make them "true" victims. His focus is on capacity, not only of the child's inability to protect themselves but also, conversely, that adults *can* protect themselves and therefore are less "true" victims. In the second quote, Officer Michael similarly points not only to the decision-making capacity of the child but also to the subject position of children in relation to their assailants. A relational understanding indicates that, as Michael and many other officers suggest of adult victims, children have events of victimization happen *to* them, and some adult sex crime victims may *contribute*, in some capacity, to the event that resulted in their victimization. Such an interpretation supports the structural underpinnings of victim-blaming beliefs that continue to shape societal perceptions of sexual violence victims. This relational understanding has implications for how child and adult sex crime victims interpret their justice outcomes:

Samantha: I truly believe if there's true victims out there it's kids. I know that adults can be and I never want to downplay an adult being a victim of a crime, but, with child victims, a lot of times we just see that where they come from. They don't have a lot at home and there's just so many other struggles that I just wanna have a chance to be their voice, and make sure that that process happens in the best way possible for them.

Trevor: The victims as children are very hard 'cause you see the aftermath. . . . They're the most—they're the ones that I feel—they're the true victims in the sense that they're completely blameless by society or anyone that would want to judge them and they're the true victims and those are the most satisfying when you get a conviction or plea deal on those.

Samantha, while never denying victim status to adults, is more concerned with the procedural standing of children and the need to make sure the criminal justice system adequately serves them. Whereas Trevor, in his recognition of children as blameless, derives satisfaction from justice being served through the formal (and swift) recognition of the perpetrator's criminal acts. He describes taking satisfaction in knowing that someone who has sexually and physically (and thus psychologically) violated a child—the "true victim"—is convicted of such acts and held accountable within the systems of justice.

Whereas child victims are interpreted as being "true" and blameless victims, there was a converse category of not ideal or less-than-true in status sex crime victims among police officers. These individuals are interpreted as neither true nor ideal victims, either because of legal barriers preventing the confirmation of their victim status or because their lifestyles and decision-making may confound the ability to support their sexual victimization. In the former, "unfounded" victim reports include those that are perceived as being unlikely to be substantiated beyond a reasonable doubt. Unfounded victim status can occur for a multitude of reasons but, in many cases, is tied to the officer's interpretation that they lack the ability to lay a charge that will stick in court, even though they may believe the victim's claims are authentic.

Joanna: [S]ometimes you have to question the validity of the information. It's frustrating because even when you did the disclosure, you still have to try to corroborate it somehow, which is next to impossible to do. . . . I guess the biggest difficulty is trying to corroborate what they are saying because you believe them, but belief isn't always enough in my job; you have to be able to have something to support it. In the section that I deal with in particular, sexual abuse, it is not like any other crime. It is not happening out in the public. There may be forensic evidence when there is intercourse, but typically it [the crime] may be touching and things like that, like fondling there is not [forensic evidence]. It is very difficult to prove. That is something I really struggled with . . . victims have a really hard time with that. They think, "well I came in here and I did a lot of really hard work talking to you about this," some of the most intimate personal details that they will ever disclose to anybody, and they expect us to go out and make an arrest on it. Very rarely have we. . . . You feel like "I believe you and I really feel that this has happened, but you need something to support it."

As the officer explains, they believe there is no genuine way to show with evidence that most nonconsensual sexual assaults occurred, despite believing the disclosure made by the victim is truthful. The officer also expresses the feeling of being caught between what she would hope to be able to do for the victim and the legal boundaries of the justice system. The victim's status is then unfounded, not because of a personal lack of credibility, but because of their ostensible inability to support their claim in a way that the police believe will overcome the legal standard of reasonable doubt (Spencer et al. 2018). In such cases, it is interpreted as unfeasible, even impossible, to prosecute a perpetrator within the scope of police investigative parameters, juxtaposed with the standards of evidence and due process that are felt to shape the profession.

The latter notion of a less-than-ideal victim includes the unfound-able victim. The unfound-able victim refers to someone who reports a sexual assault and whose credibility is difficult to legally ensure or someone who is perceived as untruthful. Unfound-able victims are those who police may find challenging to support professionally because their claims cannot be substantiated beyond the standard of reasonable doubt or because their actions evoke misgivings and call into question the feasibility of the reported incident of victimization. Alternatively, the reported sex crime of the victim may be "unfound-able" in that the victim's credibility is difficult to legally ensure. Credibility, unfortunately, can be compromised by diverse lifestyle characteristics that make the position of the victim difficult to articulate within the victim-blaming structures that are institutionally and culturally grounded (i.e., behaviors that are thought to cloud the ability to confidently assert consent was absent). In the following excerpt, Audrey indicates characteristics that she feels comprise bad lifestyles:

> **Audrey:** I would say the most difficult part of my job is dealing with individuals that have endeavoured on very bad lifestyle choices and bad things have happened to them as a result. The difficulty is some of those victims are unconscious when things happen, by reason of cocaine injection, excessive alcohol use, lifestyle choices as far as prostitutes and whatnot, not saying that they don't deserve the utmost in police service but it's very difficult piecing together events that have occurred when somebody's unconscious and when they're with other individuals that aren't strong advocates of the police and justice system.

For Adam, lifestyle choices involve a combination of factors that, when added up, can be interpreted as questioning the degree of one's victim status. In essence, the victim becomes unfound-able because there is no way to confidently confirm that they did not consent prior to their use of illegal substances or prior to losing consciousness. Due to their lifestyle choices, they are not interpreted as victims of sexual violation; instead, they are interpreted as unable to credibly verify that the sexual acts were nonconsensual. In consequence, this bars their positioning as the ideal or true victim and, instead, evidences a causal relationship between poor lifestyle choices and forms of sexual victimization that parallels conventional forms of discrediting (Goffman 1963). The result is the construction of the unfound-able victim through a form of victim blaming. Alcohol and drug consumption become factors that distort the recall of a sexually violent narrative, and because of the relationships formed through consumption practices, victims are interpreted as less than ideal because they have made seemingly compromising decisions when choosing associates. The victims either personally bear or are linked to individuals who bear the stigma of addiction (Goffman 1963), and even if they are not a drug user, they are likely stigmatized by association (Ricciardelli and Moir 2013). Beyond, and perhaps a derivative of, choices and associates, unfound-able victims are also less often interpreted as believable.

> **Hilary:** There is also a little frustration to, this is probably not nice this is going to sound . . . we do get people . . . who I don't feel they are reporting what they are reporting for the right reasons. Is that a nice way of saying it? Or to be perfectly honest, I don't necessarily believe that they were assaulted. . . . I would still treat them no different than any other person. At the end of the day when you take the investigation totality and look at it and you truly: a) don't have evidence and b) don't believe in your heart of hearts that what is being reported even happened. But, yet, you still have to spend just as much time, effort, and resources on that particular file and not the one that you believe [that] something legitimate did happen to them.

Although unfound-able victims are more often associated with adults, youth too can be unfound-able. Participants described cases where they believe young victims either do not understand the allegations they are making about a person or they confound feeling deeply hurt by the behaviors of another person with being the victim of sexual wrongdoing. In the former, for example, officers describe instances where youth hear and repeat sexual terms (e.g., "blowjob") and use these terms to report being sexually victimized. When questioned, however, officers discover some youth incorrectly use the sexual terminology and, thus, are not victims of sexual assault; they may still be victims but not of sexual misconduct. In the following cases, officers explain instances of youth making false allegations due to underlying motives.

> **Ryan:** I'd rather deal with kids 12 and under. I know some people are like, "oh my God, you're nuts." I'd rather them because, I'd rather be able to help them young. I find 12 to 16, there's always that motive you gotta look at. I didn't get that iPad, so I'm gonna say "daddy did this kind of thing." Not that I enjoy that, it's just there's a lot more to proving that it's true, or proving that it's not true.

Christina: Not to say that it's the majority of the time, but we do find more cases with teens than with kids where there's maybe a bit more of stretching of what actually happened. So there'll be an allegation of a sexual assault. But through investigation, it's more often with teens that we will uncover that it's because they cheated on their boyfriend or they became pregnant and they didn't want their parents to find out, or there's a sort of extraneous situation that brought them to want to say what they said and make the allegation. That's not all of the time, it's just with that population the occurrence rate of that particular thing compared to kids, you know, kids just don't usually make up elaborate stories like that.

In both of these interviewee responses, the officers see reports of sexual violence by youth as subterfuge or in need of substantiation. The question of motive comes into play, often tied to the threat of a youth "getting into trouble" by their parent or "partner," as does the confusion of "hurt" with "criminality." Police consider testimony from children to be far more believable than that of adolescents and adults—not because of intellectual capacities but because of an ostensible tendency of young adults to use sexual assault reporting as a fulcrum to exact revenge or punishment on an unyielding parent or former lover. For police, the potential to bring extraneous situations into sexual assault allegations as a motivator is what separates youth from child sex crime complainants. Despite the evaluation of adult sex crime victims' decision-making capacity, lifestyles, associates, and ability to engage in subterfuge, victims remain responsible for demonstrating the validity of their claims. For investigators, this challenge is what conjoins the unfounded and unfound-able victim statuses. Such responsibilization is revealed in the following responses:

Isaac: A couple of women are downtown and they maybe [are] having some drinks. No issues with that. And they walk home. And one of them maybe decided to walk by themselves. And they get attacked because they're walking by themselves. I, in all my years of policing, when you're dealing with someone you may say, you may give them some orders, like, "I wouldn't recommend that."

Deborah: A lot of our victims, if they don't get the help at a younger age, they pop up like non-stop. I think I've had the same victim at least three, four times. Like a few of them. And it's kind of one of those educational pieces where if we can make them understand at a younger age that it's not okay to be, and it's okay to say "no," and get out of that situation before it happens, then it's not one of those [situations where you] have a victim . . . they come forward and next thing you know there's like a parade of people that have victimized them. And they just lack education.

Uriah: [Referring to a case where a teenage boy distributed a sexual video that was privately shared with him by a teenage girl.] [The victim] was dumb enough to make a movie—whether you asked or didn't ask—but she sent it to you. And you decided to share it, like [something] every one of us 15-year-old boys would have done. Because people just forget. People forget what it's like to be a kid. [. . .] When that 15-year-old boy gets it, he's responsible for it, too. And he needs to have a talking to, to understand how he now has to be responsible for that, but you can't ever tell that boy you're wrong to ask [for the movie]. [. . .] My educational conversation with that girl and her parents would be an hour and a half. My conversation with that boy and his parents was 10 minutes.

As evinced across these excerpts, some officers perceive victims as bearing much of the responsibility for the risk of victimization. Within this context, less-than-ideal victims can be seen, in part, as failing to take the necessary precautions to protect themselves. For Isaac, particular circumstances are inherently risky and, perhaps, reflect the limits of the sovereign state (Garland 1996). According to this officer, police can inadvertently place responsibility on individuals to reorient their comportment to protect themselves from sexual predation. In relation to Deborah's response, the responsibility for victimization is placed on victims, particularly victims who are more vulnerable to victimization for whatever reason. Central here is that these types of victims must be inculcated with the values and thinking (i.e., education) deemed more suitable for avoiding situations that ostensibly lead to victimization. It is, in this case, not a matter of managing offenders, but of making particular victims into risk managers. In the context of sexual violence committed by and against youth through photo sharing, Uriah is clearly more pessimistic regarding youth's ability to understand the implications of nonconsensual intimate image sharing. He undergirds his interpretation of nonconsensual image sharing by conceptualizing the ideal victim. In cases of sexual violence, the ideal victim is further complicated by a construct tied to gendered myths that women, especially young women, should be sexually passive, while men are seen to be inherently sexually active and free to express themselves sexually (Randall 2010). This myth often results in the interpretation of women who express themselves sexually as deserving of any harm they experience in consequence, while the men who commit this harm are simply "boys being boys" (e.g. engaging sexually, with or without consent, due to their "uncontrollable" and "natural" sexual urges).

Uriah's understanding of the ideal victim leaves very little room for forms of victimization where the victim is understood as having been consensually involved at some point but not at a later point. It creates a space for the "unfound-able" victim by compromising their credibility because of a view that consent, in such cases, cannot be fluid or subject to change. In this framework, only a small minority of sexual violence cases would ever satisfy the requirements of true victim status. Responsibilizing beliefs such as these imply that certain victims are unruly and must be inculcated with the proper morals and risk management mentalities to prevent their victimization—arguably even suggesting their victimization is not as pure as that of the "real" victim.

CRITICAL REFLEXIVITY IN POLICING

In this section, we explore precisely how particular ways of thinking among police challenge interpretations of victims and, as reflexive of a continuously changing police culture within and across organizations, detachments, and even shifts or platoons, serve as a corrective to notions of "ideal" victim-hood—notions that remain in society among civilians as well as among select officers. The institution of policing, although powerful in its ability to bind officers and guide their practices, does not exclude the potential for officers to express autonomy; officers require discretion to excel in their vocation (Goldsmith 1990). Researchers have evinced that officers express individualism by performing their policing duties in ways that reflect their personal values and understanding of their role in society and of the cultural and organizational pressures to conform to the practices within their specific police service (Brown 1988; Chan 1997). The malleability and diversification of police culture, coupled with space for individual agency within police culture (Brown 1988; Manning 2007; Paoline, Meyers, and Worden 2000), points to the discretionary power of officers to interpret and even respond to victims differently:

> **Vivian:** People think that sexual assault is . . . you're jogging in the park and you get attacked from behind and pulled into the bushes and you get quote unquote "raped" and that's not common. That's what the lay person thinks sexual assault is. People don't think sexual assault is two people who meet downtown who consent to go home with each other and may or may not have an understanding that something sexual is going to happen to them. People don't see that as sexual assault. Society wants to see a true victim, they want to see a true victim, they want to see someone who's rendered incapacitated, someone who's rendered unconscious, somebody who has no say in the circumstance that they found themselves in, like children or a person who's jogging in the woods.

> **Nigel:** I find not only defense but sometimes [the] crown will look at a lot of other behavior that maybe the victim or complainant engaged in and that affects whether that goes to trial, which I don't agree with. [. . .] [I]t's not uncommon when you're dealing with people, might be a young adult who is dealing with

drugs, or mental health issues, or behavioral problems, they're kind of going through that time in their life where they're learning things, and yet I find the victimization isn't taken as seriously.

In some cases, as shown in Vivian's response, taking a critical stance may mean reflecting on how society more generally views and constructs stereotypes about sexual assault victims. Threaded through social discourse is the need for an "ideal" victim, and it is in this context, exacerbated by the fact that police officers are members of (and thus socialized in) society and informed by such discourses, that the conceptualization can seep into police culture and structural realities that shape understandings of victimization. Vivian interprets this societal view of sexual assault as a gross misrepresentation of what constitutes sexual violence in society, which further explains how such misconceptions can fuel the underreporting of sexual victimization among those who fail to recognize they are victims. True victims, in this interpretive framework, rarely exist in society. As such, it serves as a salient corrective in guiding sexual assault investigations and opposes the Crown and others not taking a victim's claims seriously enough because they fail to hold the status of the ideal victim. Relatedly, a cohort of officers noted the contestation over sexual assault investigations and the need to educate frontline officers regarding their interpretations of sexual violence victims.

> **Jenna:** [I]n my experience, but I'll see some detectives that are very much "yep I know that this person, this is the 14th time they're reporting a sexual assault to police—there is no way this can go to court or trial, why am I wasting my time with this?" Somebody will automatically just shut down and not believing—they're lying. Oh there are inconsistencies in the statement, "done," right? And then there are others though, that will be like "oh just because they lied before makes them more vulnerable which makes them easier to offend against." You'll see both personalities kind of start to pop out a little bit.

Jenna's words show the different ways officers approach victims of sexual assault, each respective of different ways of interpreting a victim's position. She draws attention, first, to officers who question the claimant's victim status, considering it likely unfound-able, because of their history of "false" reporting. Such experiences appear to have discredited the claimant because they are deemed to be lying. Jenna, second, presents the interpretation of a claimant as even more susceptible to sexual victimization because of their discredited status (i.e., she has reported before and no one has acted upon it, thus why would the police take her claims seriously this time?). Her reflective process shows the diversity in officers' approaches to sexual violence and the role of the ideal victim in shaping their approach. The less-than-ideal victim is easily discredited, and as such, investigative hours spent on their case can appear futile and unrewarding. Some officers attribute the officers' questioning of a victim's report to a need for officers to be more educated about what constitutes sexual victimization and how to ensure victims feel respected and heard—despite their personal interpretations of the victim and their situation.

> **Randy:** A couple of months ago, I had an officer who refused to transport a person to the hospital for a sexual assault examination. And I'm like, "that's not your call, you take the person, you're investigating a sexual assault." It's kind of putting the cart before the horse, right? You haven't come to the end so you can't conclude it and say that it's unfounded and that they should be charged with public mischief—which it shouldn't have been the case in that investigation, anyways. But when the person is saying that they've been sexually assaulted, and you are investigating a sexual assault and they're asking to be taken for medical care to the hospital, then you take them to the hospital. Right? So you just run the gambit of everything. . . . Somehow they can investigate an assault or an aggravated assault but if you put sex in front of it, it blows everybody's mind. All of a sudden they're thinking all sorts of crazy things, not collecting evidence, looking at the person as if it's a—like how much I like this person and how much I believe this person rather than what evidence is there and that's really what we're asking. Just focus on what evidence you can find and those very basic things.

Randy's words clearly highlight points of officer intervention in a sexual assault case that counteract police use of discretion and thus traditional police culture; she describes how all victims need to be treated with respect and deserve the full "gambit" of services. Further, she highlights the residual victim blaming that may compromise the level of investigative care victims experience. In response, officers clearly need to look beyond the sexual element of the offense when investigating and responding to such crimes. The gravity of not adequately responding to sexual assaults, including the serious health implications for those sexual violence victims who do not receive much-needed medical attention, is undeniable.

DISCUSSION

Here, in chapter 4, we demonstrate that variation (perhaps extreme) exists among police interpretations of victims of sex crimes. We show that these statuses are based on the interpretation that child victims are "true" or "ideal victims" and other victims (i.e., youth and adults) tend to occupy a less-than-ideal victim status. Police interpretations of victim status, we show, are focused on capacity, not only of the child's inability to protect themselves but also, conversely, of the adult's capacity to do so, and this capacity makes adults (and youth) less "true" victims. Such statuses are rooted in perceived legal challenges (i.e., police interpretations that the case is unlikely to meet the standard of guilty beyond a reasonable doubt) and beliefs about victims' believability based on lifestyle or other social stereotypes about sexual assault victims.

Less-than-ideal victims may be deemed as such due to not having "good" associates or making "good" choices. As a result, these victims are partially responsibilized for their victimization or are not believed at all—potentially in response to structural and systemic processes that impose a sense of lacking credibility on the victim due to their current or past actions or lifestyle choices (among other reasons). Overall, these less-than-ideal victims, for no fault of their own, are seen as making police work more difficult because their lifestyles, identities, or the circumstances of their victimization complicate investigations, making them more time consuming and a criminal conviction less likely due to widely held myths about the nature of sexual violence. The combination of large investigative workloads and the under-prosecution of sex crimes, specifically difficulties tied to securing a conviction in most sex crime investigations, may leave some officers believing that only "ideal victims" are worth the investigative efforts. Thus, we encourage future researchers to focus on how the goal or institutional pressures for convictions versus victim treatment may influence police interpretations of victims of sex crimes and what constitutes appropriate responses to these victims.

In contrast to the discussion of "true" victims described by many officers, a cohort of officers were critical of sexual violence stereotypes and described progressive approaches to policing based on ensuring procedural fairness for all complainants of sex crimes. Officers that expressed criticisms of stereotypes regarding sexual violence may be more equipped to provide nonjudgmental care rather than responsibilizing advice as they rebuff the use of stereotypes and victim blaming. These officers balance their occupational role—with its legal parameters and with structural protocols shaping investigations—with victim needs. Although we cannot be sure to what extent their critical beliefs map onto their everyday practices, they may find ways to give voice to victims while being fully aware that, legally, they are unlikely to secure a conviction. In line with critical victimology, we emphasize how change can emerge in an organizational context through the exercise of agency of actors in these settings. Overall, we show through an analysis of police interpretations of problems related to sexual violence that this can be the basis of the emergence of new policing practices and the influence of feminist activism around sex crimes.

Chapter 5

Collaborative Policing and Networked Responses to Victims of Sex Crimes

Since the early 1990s, Western states are increasingly favoring collaborative and networked forms of governance, including those relating to the management of crime (Brewer 2013; Crawford 1997, 2006; Garland 1996). Crawford (1997, 4) describes this networked approach as "a dispersed and fragmented web of networks and 'partnerships,' in which interests of the state collide with local power élites, established agencies, charitable bodies, private businesses, and representatives of other organized groups." Loader (2000) contends that police networks are fragmented and pluralized, which can blur agents' roles and responsibilities and create overlap in practices within institutions. Such descriptions raise questions about how amorphous, fragmented bodies of governance operate, and how the pluralization of policing functions coexists with the objectives of potentially competing agencies.

The literature on the networking of police with other agencies/institutions is fairly extensive, particularly as it probes the divergence of techniques of governance, surveillance, and punishment (Cohen 1985; Dean 2010; Garland 2001; Rose 2000; see, e.g., Simon 2007). For example, in the mid-1990s Rose (1996) used the phrase "governing through community" to describe the mobilization and instrumentalization of the community into techniques and programs of governance. Haggerty and Ericson (2000, 611) identify the growth in formations of surveillant assemblages in which there is a coming together of various professionals (police, social workers, health workers, educators, etc.) and of the knowledge compiled within each particular institution. The engagement of police and other state security agencies with community organizations has been categorized as the growth of the punitive state (Cohen 1985; Garland 2001) and the "securitization" of state and society (Hallsworth and Lea 2011). These assessments focus on the punitive roles of "the criminal justice institutions that adjudicate and sanction criminal wrong-doing" (Beckett and Murakawa 2012, 221). Within these frameworks of analysis, little to no attention is given to how networked policing and police partnerships are mobilized to support victims of crime, particularly child victims and their families.

National and international governing bodies have long recognized that responding to child victims requires a multisectoral approach involving social workers, educators, medical professionals, and police, among others (e.g., World Health Organization 2006). Thus, police investigate child sexual assault and serious cases of abuse but are also mandated to share information with child welfare agencies (e.g., Ontario's Child and Family Services Act 2007, s. 72; Alberta's Child, Youth and Family Enhancement Act 2000, s. 5) and, in some jurisdictions, to conduct joint investigations (e.g., "A Coordinated Response to Child Abuse Investigative, Justice and Community Services for the City of Kingston and Frontenac County" [Kingston Frontenac Anti-violence Coordinating Committee 2009]; "Protocol between the London Police Service and the Children's Aid Society of London and Middlesex" [London Police Service and Children's Aid Society 2002]).[1] To illustrate, an estimated 85,440 substantiated child maltreatment investigations occurred in Canada in 2008, of which 3 percent (2,607) were identified as primarily sexual abuse (Public Health Agency of Canada, 2008, 3). Of these cases of sexual abuse, a joint investigation between police and child protection services responded to about 55 percent (Tonmyr and Gonzalez 2015, 133).

Yet although multidisciplinary interventions have the potential to provide holistic care for victims and their families, the efficacy of collaborative ventures can be impeded by variances in procedures, by different emphases on priorities for action between agencies, and by the potentially conflicting goals of preserving evidence and supporting children and families (Newman and Dannenfesler 2005; Sedlak et al. 2006). If police are generally committed to augmenting support for victims of crime, particularly child victims, yet frustrated by the challenges of networked responses, how do they navigate these tensions? How do networked responses reify and/or disrupt the traditional police roles and responsibilities of responding to and investigating crime involving child victims?

In this chapter, we examine the networking of Canadian police agencies with governmental and nongovernmental organizations in response to child victims of sex crimes. We analyze police interpretations of collaboration, as well as their expressed perceptions of its benefits and challenges. By focusing on police investigations and responses to child victims, specifically, and examining how police organizations negotiate their partnerships with community organizations, we expose the often vague and fluctuating boundaries of roles and responsibilities between police and community partners. This fluctuation creates challenges and tension and, in some cases, can jeopardize the police's ability to successful lay charges. Yet, as we will show, police also recognize the value of support provided to child victims and their families through productive community partnerships.

NETWORKED POLICING AND CHILD ADVOCACY CENTERS

Since the late 1960s, Canadian police officers have been mandated to collaborate with other sectors in response to child maltreatment and abuse (Tonmyr and Gonzalez 2015). The movement toward the networking of police with other organizations corresponded with a broader shift, in Canada, the United States, and beyond, toward community policing. This shift expanded the scope of policing to include efforts to increase social capital through multiagency partnerships with social welfare agencies (McCarthy 2013). Various groups and individuals also became involved in "sharing information, keeping records, making plans, setting targets, establishing networks for the surveillance and documentation" (Rose 2000, 333). Such partnerships have the potential to foster communication and collaboration, yet international scholarship of the 1980s and 1990s characterized police partnerships as rife with tension (Bullock, Tilley, and Erol 2006). Crawford (1997, 60) suggests "the reality of competition, conflict, and organizational autonomy remain essential characteristics of criminal justice" and community policing networks. Although police are generally supportive of community partnerships and working relationships with agencies in the context of working with child victims (O'Neill and McCarthy 2014; Finkelhor, Wolak, and Berliner 2001), they still must navigate the tensions of such collaborations.

One identified area of tension in police partnerships is the lack of a clear chain of command in partnership processes (O'Neill and McCarthy 2014). Another notable tension lies in police perceptions of "social work" skills as inferior to traditional crime-fighting skills (McCarthy 2013). Reiner (2000) describes traditional policing as involving use of force, excitement, and risk, as well as the conduit for displays of masculinities and solidarity with fellow officers. Police collaboration with community agencies calls for a role change in policing that departs from this traditional model. The reduced focus on enforcement changes the experience of policing and expectations of police (see DeJong, Burgess-Proctor, and Elis 2008). Scholars show that the integration of alternative forms of policing is highly dependent on officers' receptivity (Cross, Finkelhor, and Ormrod 2005; Lumsden 2016). For example, O'Neill and McCarthy (2014) found male officers to be more skeptical than female officers of collaborative partnerships and to evaluate partnerships in terms of clear outputs such as intelligence and cost savings as opposed to personal relationships.

Multiagency centers, such as child advocacy centers (CACs), exemplify collaboration between police and community organizations. They embody the type of *"institutional annexation* of sites and actors beyond what is legally recognized as part of the criminal justice system" (Beckett and Murakawa 2012, 222). CACs began operating in the United States in the 1980s in response to concerns that the multisectoral response to child abuse subjected child victims to "repetitive and often distressing interviews" (Herbert and Bromfield 2016, 341) and revictimized them through the criminal inves-tigative process (Cronch, Viljoen, and Hansen 2006; Hornor 2008; Hubel et al. 2014). CACs developed as community-based facilities that provide a child-friendly setting for young victims of crime to report allegations and seek assistance. They use multidisciplinary approaches to conduct forensic interviews and provide a range of services to victims, witnesses, and family members. As of 2022, there are more than nine hundred CACs in operation in the United States (National Children's Advocacy Center, nationalcac.org) and a robust body of literature examining their effectiveness and operations in America (Cross et al. 2007; Herbert and Bromfield 2016; Hornor 2008; Jones et al. 2007; Newman and Dannenfesler 2005).

Researchers note favorable outcomes, which include increases in confes-sions, child disclosures, and filed criminal charges (Faller and Henry 2000; Moran-Elis and Fielding 1996). Yet scholars have identified collaborative tensions that include conflicting priorities, interagency barriers, and prob-lems with coordination management (Faller and Henry 2000; Newman and Dannenfesler 2005; Sheppard and Zangrillo 1996). That said, Herbert and Bromfield (2016, 350) conducted a systematic review of literature on CACs and noted that the majority of studies focused on the efficacy of criminal justice outcomes such as disclosures, arrests, and convictions; child and fam-ily outcomes; or on service user satisfaction. Evaluations of CAC efficacy, however, do not consider police attitudes toward such collaborative responses to child victims of crime, or how police attitudes and perceptions of joint responses can manifest in functional ways, such as shaping processes of information sharing within the partnership.

More important, there is a grave lack of scholarship on Canadian CACs. This may in part reflect their relative novelty. It was not until 2002 that the Zebra Centre, Canada's first CAC, was created in Edmonton, Alberta. As of early 2022, there are thirty CACs/CYACs across the country, with many more in development.[2] Not only are CACs somewhat new to Canada, but their composition varies significantly. For example, the spacious Sheldon Kennedy Centre in Calgary, Alberta, has an on-site staff of close to one hun-dred people representing the police, Crown, Ministry of Health, and child services (as well as two resident trauma dogs). Yet other places with CAC designation can be simply child-friendly buildings or rooms equipped for forensic interviews that are available for use by law enforcement and child protection services, often operating with only a handful of staff. For example, Koala Place in Cornwall, Ontario, is a small, child-focused facility available to police, RCMP, and child protective services, all of which work off-site and use Koala Place primarily as a place to meet with child victims and families. These differences in CAC makeup are indicative of the wide variance of protocols—not only between provinces but also between jurisdictions and counties—regarding how and when joint investigations take place (Tonmyr and Gonzalez 2015). Variances in how the joint investigations are conducted tend to exist along a continuum of formal joint investigations (e.g., collaboration is obligatory and procedures are clearly outlined) to separate investigations (e.g., one agency is solely responsible for the investigation); within that continuum are various informal joint investigations that include some degree of collaboration (Moran-Elis and Fielding 1996; Tonmyr and Gonzalez 2015).

Reflecting on the changing shape of investigative practices supports that a state of transition is underway in Canada; police networking increasingly exists along a continuum that ranges from physically established advocacy centers to ad hoc negotiations. Given this range of environments for networked policing in Canada, how do police attitudes vary with regard to their roles and responsibilities in collaborative responses to child victims of sex crimes? Do these attitudes differ in respect to the presence or absence of a CAC, and how policing processes are implemented within CACs? By focusing on the management and sharing of information between partner agencies, we illuminate the complexities and practicalities of joint responses to child sexual abuse.

COLLABORATIVE POLICING IN ACTION

Our research reveals the challenges and benefits of partnerships between police and community agencies, challenges that are grouped in two themes: (1) information sharing and (2) roles and responsibilities. CACs serve to illustrate best practices in how these challenges are being addressed, particularly through memorandums of understanding that clarify policies and practices around the sharing of information and the overlapping of professional responsibilities. But, before looking at challenges and best practices, we address the role of child victim support among police agencies across Canada, and how this role fosters, and even requires, partnerships with community agencies.

The Role of Child Victim Support

Law enforcement agencies have a dual mandate of child protection and criminal prosecution (Sedlak et al. 2006). Under provincial and territorial legislation such as Alberta's Protection against Family Violence Act and Ontario's Child, Youth and Family Services Act, police have the authority to assume child protection measures such as taking children to "a place of safety." Several officers described the goal or mandate of their unit as simply "protecting kids," a mandate primarily realized through criminal prosecution. Officers suggest other professionals in the community best handle the thera-peutic aspects related to victim support:

> **Brianna:** We do the investigations. . . . [W]e're not social workers, we're not. We're detectives.

> **Donald:** There's all kinds of services out there. There's a child treatment center. There's all kinds of stuff that we can refer the people to. . . . We're not the pro-fessionals and they need somebody else.

By differentiating between "professionals" and themselves, officers are reify-ing their primary role as one of investigating crime. Yet police recognize the multiple and complex needs of victims and rely on this network of profes-sionals to address these needs in ways they cannot. Although delineations between jobs for professionals and police were consistently expressed, many participants identified an increased emphasis on victim support within their own agencies. Several officers expressed that police should present them-selves within the community as *more* than criminal investigators. One child abuse investigator explained:

> **Diana:** We are responsible for plugging them in somewhere. Somebody has to take that person and give them what they need in the community. So, I find as a police service that has fallen on us because we are usually the first person on scene. We are triaging everybody.

Diana suggests her job is to investigate child sexual abuse, "triage" victims, *and* connect them to community resources. She described acting as a service coordinator, noting that she would call victims to remind them of appoint-ments or to encourage them to connect to a particular service, actions that clearly go beyond the role of investigating the crime. She evinces how the increased emphasis on victim support is adding to police responsibilities, even when diverting actual therapeutic labor to community partners (e.g., the officer took on an administrative role). Another officer suggested that during any investigation, police should conduct themselves in a supportive, empathetic manner—conduct not necessarily perceived as central to police investigative functions.

> **Brenda:** I think in this role, and wearing this uniform, whether we like to admit it or not—we all like to say it's just a job—it carries a lot of weight and a lot of responsibility . . . you can sit with them and be human.

The phrase "sit with them and be human" is striking since Brenda was suggesting that officers have traditionally approached victims of crime in a detached manner, treating them as "less human." She suggests this could be mitigated with a more empathetic approach. Like others, she perceived the responsibilities of police officers as evolving to become more supportive of victims, describing this as a "huge shift" in attitudes and approaches. This trend toward victim support was noticeable across our research sites, whether or not police organizations were affiliated with a CAC.

CHALLENGES AND TENSIONS
WITHIN PARTNERSHIPS

Police officer respondents were unanimous in their willingness to refer victims to community partners for psychological, physical, legal, and emotional supports. Appreciation of community partnership and collaboration, however, varied among respondents when it came to discussing how information is, and should be, shared among agencies. Additionally, several officers expressed frustration about partnerships when they felt their own roles and responsibilities were being compromised.

Overlapping or Conflicting Roles

Direct collaboration with community organizations was most frequently mentioned with regard to working with child protection agencies, such as the Children's Aid Society (CAS).[3] Officers who described these relationships as strained often attributed it to a lack of clarity about each other's roles and expectations. Police officers' objective is to deploy investigation techniques, whereas agencies like CAS prioritize providing support and care for child victims. One respondent suggested police and CAS have traditionally operated "as two separate organizations" that historically "bump heads" (Bradley, no CAC affiliation).

Some sex crime investigators articulated a deep frustration with what they interpret as a lack of respect for protocol by the local child protection agency. A child abuse investigator explains:

Lauren: There's a few [child protection agency workers] that completely over-step what their role is. Like if you have a disclosure in a child, and 99% of the time under 16, discloses to you, it's not, "I'll deal with it," or "I'm gonna see if it's true," or "I'm gonna look into it myself." It's like get on the phone and call us. . . . And I find that's lacking.

Police officers commonly expressed a sense of ownership in the process of investigation. When CAS staff attempt their own investigations, such as by talking to children to see if allegations of abuse are true, several respondents said their own processes were undermined. Even when investigations are done in partnerships, some officers expressed frustration about working jointly with child protection agencies. One described how CAS approaches to interviews jeopardized her own process:

Brenda: I've actually had to pull them aside saying, "you can't say that. You can't say that to a parent, that you know, [the police are] gonna put 'em [in] jail forever," you know. Like it's, you can't! You know what I mean? Like know your boundaries!

The call to "know your boundaries" clearly reveals that this officer felt her boundaries were being infringed upon by the partner agency. Respondents suggested police objectives and processes for acquiring the evidence needed to lay a charge through investigative techniques have the potential to be jeop-ardized through community partnerships. This is not to say that the police are not empathetic to victims, but rather some see their role in responding to crime as a technical one. They are to gather and provide information that strengthens the potential for a conviction to protect the victim and the com-munity at large. Not surprisingly, several officers expressed preference for collaboration scenarios where they remain in full control and can ensure their own protocols are followed.

Much of the unease, and occasional expressions of animosity, heard in interviews about joint responses came from police units that do not have memorandums of understanding with child protection agencies or other com-munity members, and especially those that are not operating in an established or shared-location CAC. There was a noticeable contrast in how officers spoke of their working relationship with child protection agencies among units with formalized agreements versus those operating on an ad hoc basis. Erica, an officer affiliated with an off-site CAC, described the improvements in collaboration after senior leadership from her police unit and from the local child protection agency worked together to develop a process through which officers and child social workers meet to discuss cases and keep each other informed:

Erica: I felt that we were really bridging the gap. They [child protection agency] kind of have their own policy and procedures, and we have our own. A lot of times people who are not really familiar with the Criminal Code of Canada and the high standards you need to lay a criminal charge, would look at some of the investigations and would look at why, how could you not charge someone? So it was better to sit one-on-one, and sit with their higher-ups, to explain that to them so they could bring it back to other staff. I think that really helped.

This response illustrates the recognition that child protection agencies and police organizations have different mandates, policies, and procedures and that each organization may not understand the other's mandate. It also reflects a common misconception; child protection agencies may expect police to convict or charge an individual because these agencies lack an understanding of the burden of proof that police must establish to lay charges. In relation to Erica's response, open dialogue between police officers and child protection agencies allows officers the opportunity to explain why criminal charges could not be laid in a particular case, thus alleviating frustration on the part of both organizations. Consistently, we found that, at sites in which collaborative tensions have been (or are being) addressed, police are much more likely to express positive opinions of joint work with partner agencies, particularly in key areas such the sharing of sensitive information.

Information Sharing with Child Protection Agencies

Collaborative relationships generate the need for the sharing of confidential information among police and various agencies, organizations, and institutions. This creates challenges particularly in cases of highly sensitive information related to sexual and interpersonal violence (Gamache 2012, 884). Notably, providing victims with information about local resources (counseling, child services, etc.) was portrayed as fundamentally distinct from providing local resource partners with information about victims, alleged offenders, and criminal investigations. In the former, police simply pass on publicly available resources, such as through the distribution of a flyer or a business card. In relation to the latter, the information is not publicly available but has been generated from criminal investigation. Sharing of this information is seen as a potential threat to the investigation process, even while police recognize that to protect children it is often necessary to reveal sensitive intelligence to community partners. There is a delicate balance between the protection of children's safety and the need to follow strict investigative, security, and privacy protocols.

Although police are at times reluctant to share information with community partners, they rely on the willingness of community partners to share information with them. Many police officers identified community agencies as the primary avenue through which cases of child sexual abuse are reported. The following interview excerpt expresses a common description of how child-related cases come to the police.

> **Randy:** With children a lot of the times we get a call from the Children's Aid Society. So it's been reported to them and then they need help from the police to investigate. I'd say most of the time with kids it's through the CAS.

In addition to the CAS, Randy notes that other community partners who inform police of alleged child sexual interference include schools, hospitals, and counseling agencies. In this regard, community partners function as the information providers, initiating an investigative process through which the police proceed to gather more information in order to process an investigation.

Despite the consensus that CAS is the main source of referrals, several police officers express that child protection agencies are not always forthcoming in providing information to police, or they delay informing police in order to pursue their own investigation. Given that the primary role of police is to investigate allegations of crime, failures by CAS to report allegations of abuse to police can be interpreted as generating risk for police and the broader community.

> **Brianna:** It is a liability. There is a lot of risk attached to that in both ways, you know. Us not sharing information with them and letting them know a child is involved in a case, if someone forgets to send that email to them. And same with them, if they're not notifying us about on-going issues (no CAC affiliation).

The concerns expressed by this officer were typical of those working within organizations without a CAC affiliation and without established protocols of information sharing. Belief that community partners were withholding information was, not surprisingly, associated with reluctance to share their own investigative findings. Nonetheless, there is a recognition that the partnership between police and child protection agencies requires a two-way transfer of information. Police are recipients of information from child protection agencies and are mandated to share information; they inform child protection agencies about situations where children may be unsafe, neglected, or abused. Child protection agencies follow up on this information, conduct assessments of the home environment, and can even remove children from a home deemed unsafe.

Information, however, is not simply pieces of data transferred from one organization to another. The quality of information, including its provenance and reliability, frequently comes under scrutiny. Police may rely on receiving information from other organizations, but they expressed a degree of distrust about that information, which suggests certain ambivalence about its actual value. This was especially evident with regard to the forensic interviews of children where police must follow very strict rules and must not be perceived to lead the child in any way. Child protection agencies, schools, and other community partner organizations do not share the same protocols and procedures. An officer explained:

> **Erica:** Sometimes I have had cases where I don't feel confident laying a charge because you look at the form of questioning beforehand, or you might see an interview from Children's Aid and it's a bunch of leading questions which resulted in allegations. So that's something I think we need to look at or work on. . . . [T]hat's something we'd have to talk to these people at different agencies like schools and Children's Aid and try to interview these people [the child victims] first before these interviews get tainted so to speak.

Erica refers to the challenges of using interviews completed by community agencies or practitioners (i.e., teachers, social workers) for their own investigations because these organizations do not follow police protocols or have the same threshold of burden of proof. As a result, children must be interviewed again by police and potentially are retraumatized. Other officers suggested that, at this point, it is already "too late"; the investigation has already been undermined by what they perceived as leading questions on the part of community organizations.

Despite the tensions several police interviewees expressed, many demonstrated a commitment to collaborative relationships and offered examples of how they attempt to mitigate the possibilities that an investigation will be compromised through collaborative engagement. For example, police may conduct interviews themselves according to their protocols but allow child protection agency workers to be present or to follow the interview from the observation room or through a video feed. Police officers were most likely to describe established processes and protocols for information sharing within the context of CACs.

Child Advocacy Centers

CACs are designed to "provide a coordinated approach to addressing the needs of child and youth victims and/or witnesses in the criminal justice system" (Department of Justice 2016). CACs vary in composition, but all are equipped for forensic interviews and have adopted measures to make the interview process more comfortable and safer for children, such as using home-like furniture and play areas to foster a sense of security for child victims. An officer described an off-site CAC used for meeting with families and interviewing children, "the room the family sits in is nicer than most people's living rooms at home: big screen TV, computer, games, everything" (Brian). Other commonly described features of both on-and off-site locations were civilian dress for police officers and a general atmosphere that resembles a community center more than a police unit. Simply put, each CAC is designed to be "a safe place for kids to come to tell their story" (Stephen). In describing their local CAC, police officers typically draw a contrast between its environment and that of their police station.

> **Jeremy:** Used to be where we'd have our kids come into the lobby. They'd be paraded through the police station. . . . They'd be interviewed here, and then paraded back into the lobby—just not a good situation. Now we go down to [the CAC]. It's child friendly; it's safe; it's confidential. It's quiet, private.

This description demonstrates the advantages of an advocacy center, which include the friendly, secure, and private location, posited in contrast to the potentially distressing atmosphere of a police station. Descriptions of improvements brought about through CACs, particularly when compared with how police investigations operated prior to or without them, were common among the respondents.

> **Samantha:** The center is basically the place for the child to come and they are here to have their medical exam, they're here for therapy, they're here to see a detective, they're here for child family services. If they have to meet with the Crown before they go to court, they come here and meet with the Crown— everything is done here so this is a safe place for the kid to come.

Such descriptions of efficacies and co-located services are consistent with research in the United States that notes CACs have better facilities for child-friendly interviews and a greater commitment to joint processes (Newman and Dannenfesler 2005; Sheppard and Zangrillo 1996).

Although the aesthetics of advocacy centers are helpful for fostering a sense of security in child victims, their effective operation still depends upon collaboration between the various agencies on site. Many officers explained that the key to their success is the sharing of information and resources:

> **Stephen:** It's honestly the collaboration that happens here, it, it makes it, it makes it easy. . . . You can't operate in those, those silos anymore. It's just, it's ineffective, right? It's time consuming, it's frustrating, and it's costly.

> **Samantha:** We don't ever want to duplicate existing services. And because we're a community-based child advocacy center, we want to use that wealth of experience and networks within our community.

These officers' words illustrate not only the expanse of services made available to child victims through co-located advocacy centers but also officers' perceptions of the benefits and the efficacy of the collaboration emblematic of CACs. Child victims of sex crimes benefit by having access to multiple services, and police benefit by drawing on the knowledge and experience of partner agencies. Several officers working in CAC contexts noted they reach out to community partners when they have questions about a particular file. This suggests that, although police still focus primarily on their role in criminal investigations, they recognize that the role of other organizations overlaps with their own and can make their work more efficient. Respondents were much more likely to volunteer positive accounts of information sharing and collaborative work in on-site CACs as compared with off-site CACs and, to an even greater degree, than with units not affiliated with CACs.

The sharing of information and the development of multiagency responses to victims improve police function and can mitigate the tensions and challenges we've identified here. One officer likened the process of information sharing at his CAC to emergency room triage:

> **David:** Every morning at 9 a.m. we will triage those matters and identify what is the approach. So there may not be a police approach, but there may be a Child and Family Services approach. Or maybe it's determined that the best course is just therapy for the child. But, everybody comes to the table and offers a piece of that puzzle. . . . We are just so good at information sharing, and that is the key to our success . . . our interest is what is best for that child.

David confirms information sharing as a key to success in investigating and responding to sex crimes committed against children. He also notes that not all child protection and safety matters go through criminal justice processes. Unsurprisingly, clear communication between the various stakeholders involved allows organizations to work together rather than at cross-purposes.

Certainly, CACs are not the panacea for all collaborative challenges, and few have the benefit of co-located staffing. Officers working in on-site CACs described established protocols and practices for information sharing, such as the triage process David describes. In contrast, officers in agencies with no CAC affiliation, or with a loose affiliation to an off-site center, often referred to collaborative tensions that arise as organizations navigate the boundaries of their own roles and protocols with those of their partners. Yet even at an on-site location, one officer noted that "the hardest part is just the politics," explaining that, while "everyone wants to do what's best for the child," some organizations have stricter policies than others. As noted, how organizations share information, although certainly facilitated by having shared locations and memorandums of understanding, can still be restricted by conflicting organizational protocols, different management procedures, and distrust. Nonetheless, the identification of CACs as being in the best interest of child victims was unanimous among research participants, although many drew attention to lack of secure funding,[4] and others called for a "standardized process" for CACs across Canada.

DISCUSSION

In this chapter, we examined the complexity of police collaborative relationships with community agencies and how these relations contribute to the shaping of police responses to child victims of sex crimes. Given part of our focus in this research was on police networking more broadly, we asked interviewees about specific protocols and mandates around joint investigations and relationships to external organizations. In relation to police response to child sex crime victims, we consistently found that police are aware of the need for supports for child victims and their families and accept that part of their role is to connect victims to these supports. The extent these efforts take time away from the primary tasks involved in criminal investigations varied among officers and organizations, often dependent on the degree to which collaboration was formalized (e.g., if through established CACs). Individual police organizations and the character of the relationships with community partners also inform how and where officers invest their labor. Few officers were willing to take on therapeutic support for child victims themselves, but the majority of officers in this study expressed appreciation for the community services to which they can refer child victims and their families. Such findings are consistent with those of scholars in the United States—specifically that within police organizations "soft" police functions are kept at the margins and "hard" functions, such as criminal investigations, are prioritized (McCarthy 2013; Rabe-Hemp 2009). Officers viewed these community supports as distinct from other services police provide but fundamental to child victims.

The reification of traditional police response to crime (namely, the investigation of crime and laying of charges) is illustrated through the discussion of referrals. Processes of referral to other services allow police to delineate the boundaries of their role (e.g., police conduct criminal investigations, and community organizations provide social services). When talking about referrals, police were almost unanimously positive, although several lamented that community organizations tend to lack funding, have long wait lists, or that there were insufficient organizations within the community to refer victims (particularly in small urban centers). Referral type of collaboration does not require police to share information with community organizations, as publicly available information about services is simply provided to victims. Some police organizations have units within or attached to their organization that act as hubs to help victims navigate the various services and the criminal justice processes. This allows investigators and detectives to focus their efforts on investigative matters and hand over victim support to others. Again, this type of collaboration serves to reinforce the police role as primarily focused on criminal investigations and security. At the same time, police expressed a recognition that they were doing more for victims of crime than in previous years, even if by simply investing more effort in facilitating community referrals. Thus, the expansion of policing roles to be more supportive of crime victims was a consistent finding during our research processes.

Many positive practices result from police collaboration, but challenges still exist during collaboration between agencies with different objectives. This was most evident when boundaries or protocols were not clearly established or were interpreted as being violated by one of the parties. In contrast to simply referring child victims and their families to community services, working jointly with community organizations (such as when interviewing victims and determining a course of action) was much more likely to cause tension. Researchers, indeed, have long identified joint interviews as the main source of conflict between police and child protection services (Lloyd and Burman 1996). Police identified many of the same challenges noted in US and UK scholarship on CACs and collaborative responses to child sex abuse, such as conflicting priorities and communication difficulties (Faller and Henry 2000; Newman and Dannenfesler 2005). Yet at the same time, the majority of police respondents recognized that collaborative approaches with community partners can actually assist them in performing their role. Whether police perceive collaboration as assisting or impeding their duties depended significantly on how clearly processes of communication were defined, such as through memorandums of understanding for information sharing and joint responses to child abuse and sexual interference, a finding echoed by other researchers studying joint responses (Cross, Finkelhor, and Ormrod 2005; Jones et al. 2007). Officers in sites where collaboration happens on an ad hoc basis were likely to express frustration, dissatisfaction, and distrust of the community organization, and claim that these organizations did not understand the roles, mandates, and responsibilities of police. In contrast, officers operating in on-site CACs, or in a combination of on-site and off-site networking, reported improvements in investigation process and collaboration.

Although some officers acknowledge that challenges remain, including how organizations collaborate within on-site CACs, police spoke positively of the collaboration made possible in these advocacy centers, suggesting it made their own job easier and produced better results for victims.

Interviewees expressed trust toward community partners, appreciation for what they brought to the table, and reliance on them to "put together the pieces of the puzzle" when addressing complex cases of abuse and assault. Collaboration appears to work best when protocols are clearly in place and respected by all parties involved. Our research indicates that this can be facilitated by co-location and structured processes of information sharing (such as the daily "triage" meetings of partners). Given that CACs are still a recent phenomenon in Canada, and that the size and scope of CACs vary significantly, however, more research is needed to understand how to measure the efficacy of CACs in relation to their specific compositions and to what standards they are held. Building trust, establishing joint protocols, and strengthening processes of coordination require time and commitment from all involved parties (Cross, Finkelhor, and Ormrod 2005). Given the gravity of sex crimes against children, the lack of attention to ongoing implementation of CACs in Canada needs to be remedied.

NOTES

1. Mandates to conduct joint investigations vary among Canadian jurisdictions. Additionally, in some jurisdictions, sexual abuse involving extra-familial perpetrators, such as babysitters or a relative living outside the home, are directed to police, not child services.

2. Determining the number of CACs in Canada is impeded by variances in the nature of CACs (from a single-site location staffed by personnel from multiple agencies, to a room or small center utilized by off-site police, RCMP, and child protection services for forensic interviews, court support, and other victim services). As of 2022, the Government of Canada lists thirty currently funded child advocacy centers and child and youth advocacy centers across Canada (https://cac-cae.ca/organizations). Additional internet research revealed at least five more sites in operation or development.

3. Child protection agencies are known by a variety of names such as Children's Aid Society, Child and Family Services, and Child and Youth Services. Typically nonprofit and funded by provincial and territorial governments, these agencies are mandated to investigate reports or evidence of child abuse and neglect and to intervene to protect children.

4. CACs can receive funding from the Government of Canada, allocated from the federal Victims' Fund, for development and operation. To date, Alberta is the only province in Canada with legislated, sustainable funding for CACs as its Children's First Act reallocates funds from ministries including child welfare, social service, policing, and health toward CACs.

Chapter 6

Cynicism, Dirty Work, and Policing Sex Crimes

In Canada, sex crimes include digital crimes like online child sexual exploitation, nonconsensual intimate image sharing, and voyeurism, to name but a few (Branch 2017). Concomitantly, cybercrimes targeting end users are largely underreported to police by victims and in official statistics (Harkin, Whelan, and Chang 2018). In Canada, police-reported cybercrime occurrences, including cybersex crimes against children, youth, and adults, remain recorded at comparatively low levels (Statistics Canada 2014). There remains a schism between victim-reported incidents, police-reported occurrences, and the true prevalence of cyber sexual crimes (Bidgoli and Grossklags 2016). In the case of cyber sexual crimes, reporting becomes complicated by inconsistent police investigation and response to reporting (Huey and Broll 2015), lack of response by the courts, and the fact that cybersex crimes are often linked with "offline" sex crimes, sometimes making their reporting indistinguishable. In this often-complicated criminal justice terrain, the net effects are forms of cynicism that affect both the investigations of cybersex crimes as well as the law enforcement personnel themselves and their perceptions of their occupations and respective organizations.

Since Niederhoffer's (1967) *Behind the Shield*, cynicism has been a preoccupation in literature on policing. Understanding the sources and effects of cynicism is salient insofar as its implications for police officer identities, occupational satisfaction, and length of tenure in the profession (Travis and Winston 1998). We focus here on experiences and expressions of cynicism among Canadian police working in sex crime–related units. With focus on sex crime investigators, a cadre of officers heretofore insufficiently examined in relation to cynicism, we demonstrate that officer cynicism is not exclusively directed at criminalized individuals. It extends into operational and organizational aspects of police work and into officers' lived experiences outside of work. Due to their engagement in "dirty work" (Powell et al. 2014b; Dick

2005; Waddington 1999), sex crime investigators experience organizational and intraorganizational sources of cynicism in dealing with morally tainted forms of criminal offending. We examine sex crime unit members' sources of cynicism in relation to sex crimes and the digital world and explore sources of cynicism in police organizations and other branches in the criminal justice system. We examine how such cynicism seeps into relationships outside of the occupation. We show that cynicism related to police dirty work is experienced not only in relation to "front" and "back" regions (Dick 2005) but also in multiple organizational and social spheres. In this chapter, we foremostly address the implications of investigating and responding to sex crimes and the underexplored dirty work associated with policing cyber environments and the morally tainted elements of such policing tasks.

CYNICISM, DIRTY WORK, AND SEX CRIMES

Cynicism is a state of mind characterized by a distrust of others' motives. Modern cynicism, directed toward contemporary organizations, receives considerable attention in policing studies (Niederhoffer 1967; O'Connell, Holzman, and Armandi 1986; Reiner 2010) as well as studies of work and labor (Cartwright and Holmes 2006; Dean, Brandes, and Dharwadkar 1998). Studies of police cynicism examine cynicism's impact resulting from officer rank (Chan 2007; Crank et al. 1987), education (Paoline, Terrill, and Rossler 2015; MacVean and Cox 2012; Edge, Buffington, and Slemons 1980; Weiner 1974), professionalism (Burke and Mikkelsen 2005a; Carlan and Lewis 2009; Lotz and Regoli 1977; Niederhoffer 1967), and gender (Burke and Mikkelsen 2005b; Dorsey and Giacopassi 1986). In Niederhoffer's (1967) groundbreaking work, he contends that cynicism includes feelings of distrust and hostility directed toward the public, police organizations, or both. Cynicism is in opposition to professionalism among officers and produced when officers' experiences of policing fail to meet their occupational expectations. Reiner (2010) suggests that cynicism is a part of police culture that forces police to look continuously for signs of trouble. Balch (1972, 113) posits that police develop cynical attitudes from being exposed to "the very worst in life" (see also Loftus 2010; Enciso, Maskaly, and Donner 2017).

Cynicism, presented as a tool to help police cope with the stresses of police work and remain protected on duty (Edge, Buffington, and Slemons 1980), can be conceptualized as a means of mitigating, normalizing, or neutralizing some of the repugnant parts of police work (also see Ashforth et al. 2007; Kreiner, Ashforth, and Sluss 2006; Ashforth and Kreiner 1999). In response to their need for safety, officers develop a cognitive map of the world that serves as an interpretive framework. This framework is best understood as a guide for navigating the dangerous sides of life and as a justification for targeting groups who are thought most likely to be involved in illegal activities (Chan 1997; Reuss-Ianni 2011).

Against the backdrop of the negative and positive implications of cynicism, researchers note the complexity of policing organizations and the salience of understanding specific instances of cynicism within types of policing units (Crank et al. 1987; Regoli, Crank, and Rivera 1990). In this chapter, we analyze types of cynicism associated with sex crime units—namely, forms of cynicism connected to police investigations of and responses to cybersex crimes. We examine how police responses to sex crimes affect the experiences of cynicism among units tasked with investigating and responding to sex crimes against youth and adults, which we conceive of as a form of dirty work.

Dirty work implies occupational responsibilities that include dealing with "dirty" elements (Ashforth et al. 2007; Hughes 1962; Press 2021). As associations with dirt are viewed as contaminating, individuals who perform dirty work may feel the taint of what they deal with at work is rubbing off on them. For example, Huey and Broll (2015) examine how homicide investigators make sense of the tainted, taboo, or otherwise dirty parts of their work (see also Innes 2003; Press 2021). Recognizing policing as dirty work refutes the notion that policing is a glamorous or exhilarating occupation. Sex crimes, particularly against children, invoke the most powerful reactions from society, in terms of shame and disgust placed on the accused or convicted person (Ricciardelli and Moir 2013; Ricciardelli and Spencer 2017). Sex crime investigators engage with forms of work that are socially and morally tainted (Powell et al. 2014b; Dick 2005). Their dirty work involves hearing and seeing shocking and traumatizing details of a sex crime case, often multiple times, as they determine what happened. Investigations may include hours of watching and listening to video evidence of sex crimes committed against children, youth, and adults. Such dirty work results in a potential taint imposed on sex crime investigators and the view that there is something psychologically "wrong" with individuals who can engage in such work (Powell et al. 2014a, 2014b).

The morally charged nature adds a level of specificity to police cynicism among sex crime investigators. Cynicism manifests in relation to affixing abject *sexual* markers to individuals and groups external and internal to the criminal justice system. We demonstrate how multiple forms of cynicism emerge in sex crime policing as a way of mitigating, managing, and neutralizing the taint and stigma of sexual offending (see also Ashforth et al. 2007; Ashforth and Kreiner 1999). We reveal that cynicism in police dirty work is experienced in "front" and "back" regions (Dick 2005) as well as in multiple organizational and social spheres.

DIRTY WORK, CYNICISM, AND SEX CRIME UNITS

Reports of police officer cynicism directed toward those who are not part of police service organizations are commonplace within the policing literature (O'Connell, Holzman, and Armandi 1986; Reiner 2010). In the first section, we analyze the different ways officers working in sex crime–related units, all of whom engage with and rely on digital technologies for their investigations, express cynicism toward offenders, victims, and people encountered in their everyday lives outside of work. In section two, we draw attention to cynicism directed toward institutions or services within the criminal justice system, specifically as it manifests toward court processes and outcomes.

Cynicism toward Offenders, Victims, and Everyday Life

Throughout our interviews with members of sex crime units, there was a steady affirmation of cynicism directed toward the perpetrators of sexual violence against women and children. Cynicism was articulated as disgust toward the criminalized person, their intent, and their sexual acts, as well as a distrust of any perspectives or explanations that the accused conveyed in interviews. Being accused of a sex crime is tied to the cynical suggestion that the accused holds a master status that discredits his or her morals, values, and person. Additionally, working in the unit influenced cynicism in a way similar to the process that Phillips and colleagues (2012) refer to as courtesy stigma, which rubs off by mere association with the phenomenon. More jarringly, many officers noted how disgusted they were in speaking to offenders and having to perform a role in front of the offender. Some unit workers indicated that they had to engage in a subterfuge during interrogations to make the accused feel comfortable enough to open up about their actions (n=10), which can occur in cyber environments or in person. This, as these officers' words indicate here, is one of the more negative ways dirty work and cynicism are experienced:

> **Jason:** Another thing I find difficult when you actually have to sit down and you gotta talk to the offender. When you're doing your interview or your interrogation and you talk about the offenses that he or she's done, and, I find that uncomfortable. . . . You need to speak the language of the person you're talking to, right? . . . I don't know how to explain it, but after I'm done talking to an offender, I just don't, just don't feel, I don't know, clean?

> **Brian:** [The hardest part of my job is] befriending the offender and getting the confession. Once you've determined that there is an offence, and you have grounds for the charge, I want to interview and interrogate and get the confession and get the apology letter written—get that almost closure [for the victim].

So, close all the defense doors. But to do that, you befriend the offender. . . . It's disgusting . . . I hate that. That's sickening. It's disgusting.

Brittany: I am in a teen chat room [posing] as a 13-year-old girl, and none of the people talking to me were teen. They were all adult males from all over the world, [and] that was horrifying because you know that there's kids out there wanting to just chat and thinking this is fun; and they're in there and they are 13 and they do have handles like "blueflowergirl"—whatever, simple usernames—and they don't know. They think Cindy from Utah is Cindy from Utah or Bobby is 12 and not actually 38. It's horrific and I felt so gross because being my world, I was naïve; I didn't understand anything—oh, what is that? Like I played this role and he handfed me everything, and it made my skin crawl. You dirty pervert, how dare you talk to this innocent little girl? Because that's essentially what I was. I'm an innocent little girl, [and] I knew you are corrupting me.

Jason explains that, in performing the dirty work of a sex crime investigator, he must speak the language particular to the alleged offender. Dirtied by the interaction, he finds it difficult to convey the experience of "speaking the language." Interacting with the abject sullies the investigator. Brian identifies the act of befriending and attaining the "confession" from the accused as the hardest part of his job. He experiences what he describes as a "sickening" level of disgust toward the offender. Brian confronts a paradox of investigating crimes: to "catch" the accused in their offenses, he must act like he is supportive of their offense (cf. Joh 2009; Pogrebin and Poole 1993). Brittany, an internet child exploitation investigator, feels dirtied through her online interactions impersonating a little girl; she is sullied and astonished by her interactions with the child lurer. Investigators are cynical to the point that they feel that individuals who commit sex crimes cannot be believed. They are, because of their sexual proclivities, individuals who are inherently deceptive and malicious. This dirty work taints the investigator, and cynicism is a "defensive tactic" (Ashforth et al. 2007, 162) to counter such occupational taint.

Cynicism is not reserved for offenders but can be experienced in relation to victims (cf. Campbell, Menaker, and King 2015). Researchers reveal a complicated relationship between police and victims (Belknap 2010; Jordan 2008). On the one hand, cohering with the move away from the traditional crime-fighting model of policing to the service model, police organizations have made strides toward providing services for victims of crime (Loftus 2010; Koster et al. 2016). On the other hand, the literature indicates that cynical attitudes toward victims remain steadfast among sex crime investigators, who, as a way of coping with the volume of cases and emotional exhaustion, often decrease investments in relationships with recipients by emotionally distancing themselves from them. This decreased involvement is expressed by cynical attitudes toward recipients, reduced empathy, and by "blaming the victim" (Maslach, Jackson, and Leiter 1996; Schaufeli and Enzmann 1998; Bakker and Heuven 2006). The relationship between victims and the police is also complicated by the variability in who constitute and are recognized as victims. As Javaid (2017) demonstrates, victim-blaming attitudes may unleash onto certain types of victims, as police cynicism remains a core characteristic of police cultures. Within this context, blaming and credibility issues are likely to manifest themselves through negative and hostile police responses, elevating questions about deserving and undeserving victims and attributions of blame, and how the legitimacy of the victim in sex crime cases hinges on conceptions of "ideal" victimhood (Graham 2006; Christie 1986; Javaid 2015). Sexual assault cases can be further complicated by digital evidence:

> **Brenda:** I'd rather help the kids, the younger kids. The 12 to 16 ones, it's hit or miss.. . . . You know like there's different *motives* for it. Anything over 12, 16, is a lot of boyfriend-girlfriend stuff. Like it's very rare that we don't know who the predator is kind of thing, like who the accused is. . . . It's a consent issue, like whether or not they consented, or they didn't. . . . So domestic relationship, they break up, she saying he came over [and] sexually assaulted her. He's saying there's no way. I went over to see my son and then I came home. And then she's like I can give you Facebook messages. Give them to me. Well he has no problems giving them to me . . . from just reading those messages you can tell that they were basically trying to get back together, and then she finds out he's dating someone else. And it's the same time line as the allegation.

Brenda describes a scenario reflexive of a type of cynicism that continues to engender attitudes toward victims among some police. Her cynicism lies in her belief that victim motives do not align always with the stated reasons for coming forward to the police with a sexual assault allegation. Conversely, child victims are interpreted as incapable of the type of subterfuge in which youth and adults engage. They are the ideal victim (Christie 1986), not to be blamed for their victimization; they cannot consent to sexual acts, and their claims will not be contravened by digital evidence. This form of cynicism has the effect of making some victims harder to "believe" and is only further complicated by cyber components of investigations.

Police cynicism can also manifest in relation to possible targets outside the criminal justice system, such as the dirty work related to investigating cybersex crimes invading the home and social lives of police. Dirty work can make its way into the perceptions of categories of people with whom officers would inevitably engage in their everyday lives (n=44). When speaking of their experiences in their respective internet child exploitation units, respondents indicated the following:

Herman: It is not even the visual. . . . Watching a child being sexually assaulted and raped is obviously horrific, but to me the audio, hearing it, hits home, like the sound of a child um like an infant being sexually assaulted . . . to have a little girl screaming "Daddy stop," it resonates with you, you don't forget it, so carrying that with you. . . . I think it changes people.

Christina: When I first started I did I would be eating dinner and an image would pop into my head that I saw that day, and I would be like "ugh" ya got to shake it off . . . especially if you have your own children, because they'll [the child victim in the online video] be wearing the same pajamas that your kids have or something, that affects you.

Edward: I was naïve like most people are. Thinking that what child pornography is [is] naked pictures of little kids and whatever, not [explicit context removed]. I wasn't really aware of what child pornography was. . . . Does it bother me? No. Not as much. I'm a little hardened to it, but I'll tell you what it does do to you—to me anyways. . . . When I see somebody with a kid, and this is a sad thing, I don't go "look at dad playing with his kid." I go "what is he doing to his kid?" I'm suspicious of everybody with a child. Here's another thing. I've got a neighbor—he's got 3 little boys—cute little kids . . . great neighbors with great kids, and they come and I go "how's it going?" and I've become conscious that I'm not gonna touch this kid. Or, I might touch him, I might sometimes if they come and do the little tickle-thing, but I make sure dad's there and it's just a little tickle because I'm not like an uncle, I'm a friendly next-door neighbor, but I don't want to be the sicko but nobody is thinking that. . . . So, I think that's the one way that it affected me, not that it's ruining my life, but it makes you very suspicious.

Herman's response shows how particular sounds form a lasting memory that becomes folded into the lives of cybersex crime investigators. The sonorous element of videos of child sexual assault changes the investigator and has a lasting effect on their everyday lives; it "hits home." Such dirty work sullies the home life of investigators through the sights and sounds of video evidence of sexual victimization. In Christina's narrative, we see how the dirty work of sex crime investigators invades family life. She indicates that investigators become hardened to the contents of online child pornography but affirms that such investigations leave an imprint and can have lasting effects when they are connected to parenting through homologous visual artifacts, in this case children's clothing. While Edward claims that he cannot speak for everyone in his unit, the more generalized form of cynicism affected a portion of the respondents working with child, youth, and adult victims of sex crimes. His narrative reveals that his cynicism is directed toward parents and grandparents (exclusively males) *and* has a disciplining effect on his own behaviors, particularly his interactions with his neighbor's children. The suspiciousness Edward describes is widely noted among police officers (McAra and Mcvie

2005). The work environment produces suspicion in police officers, and this suspicion reinforces their cynical attitudes, as evidenced by Edward's response. Along with his cynicism toward others (especially those with children), he governs his own behaviors to ensure others do not become suspicious of him—due to his exposure to and awareness of sex-related offenses. His cynicism results in him viewing every man as, potentially, a motivated sex offender, and he seeks to ward off the possibility of being accused of such an offense. While he does not interpret this effect as particularly negative, this suspicion mitigates his relationships toward others.

Cynicism Associated with the Criminal Justice System

Police officers in sex crime units, particularly in internet child exploitation units, indicated that frontline officers and colleagues working in other units had made comments such as "I could never do that job" or "How can you look at those pictures?" This form of exceptionalism places sex crime unit personnel outside of the organizational mandates of frontline police work. The forms of cynicism experienced by sex crime unit workers are, in part, different in kind than the forms of cynicism experienced by frontline police officers. This is similar to what Kreiner and colleagues (2006) refer to as "compartmentalized stigma" where only some tasks are strongly stigmatized. They perform tasks that most police officers feel personally and professionally unable to do, which impacts how they view their dirty work and how others view their occupational role. As such, sex crime investigators are treated differently than regular duty officers. Cynicism is woven into policing through personal job satisfaction and external recognition of their work:

> **William:** There's days when I hate people . . . it's more about the work because we all know doing this work, the rewards are few and far between unless you're doing something wrong. It's never really brought to your attention if you're doing it right.

> **Jerome:** In our line of work there's nothing that's ever gratifying. People won't come to you happy and shake your hand.

For William, an internet child exploitation investigator, the feeling of never meeting the public's expectation that ostensibly does not recognize when something goes "right" is the source of cynicism. This is similar to Worden's (1995) assertion that public sentiment plays a role in determining levels of cynicism among police officers. In this instance, hate is projected onto humans (in general), and as such, cynicism becomes the basis for how one sees the world. For Jerome, his cynicism is oriented to the nature of the police work. Due to the nature of the crimes they investigate, a majority of the workers in sex crime units we interviewed indicated that they were always interacting with people at the worst moments in their lives. There seemed to be an endless number of people experiencing these "worst moments." To exemplify, an internet child exploitation investigator explained that closing one case was the equivalent to using a spoon to empty a tub that is still filling with water. These conditions can make it difficult for these personnel to create a positive identity (Ashforth and Kreiner 1999) and to find honor or nobility in their work.

Another area within the criminal justice system that invoked officer cynicism was the court. Balch (1972, 112) highlights the perceived detachment from the police and the judiciary, noting that the police often experience a great deal of frustration from plea bargain deals and become "frustrated at every turn in their efforts to win convictions." Similarly, in our study, one of the greatest sources of cynicism among officers rests in their views of the courts' ability to achieve justice (n=50). Marta, a sex crime investigator, indicates that the most disappointing part of her position is the court process:

> **Marta:** You're always building towards court if it's a charge file, and yet it's so unsatisfying for all of the participants in so many ways because people still have this kind of naïve belief, and everybody lies to everybody about that people will get justice in that court house and it's just not the case.

Justin echoes the sentiment:

> **Justin:** Child porn, I finished a case last month that was a 2013 case. They take time to do, and you have to get your mind into every time you go back into it to finish it. The testifying in court is the hardest in the sense that I have to explain how I did [the investigation] and I have to explain it usually to an older gentleman who is not text savvy. . . . Then of course, you have to deal with the defense attorneys who their job is to make you look bad.

As Justin indicates, beyond the time lag between the occurrence of the offense and the trial, the courts are poorly oriented to cybercrimes investigations. In addition, due to the antagonistic nature of criminal trials, defense attorneys smear investigators in an attempt to discredit their investigations. Marta agrees that, for most of the participants, the courts are not a space of justice but, rather, disappointment. According to a large majority of investigators in our study, they are spaces where neither offenders nor victims receive justice (n=50). In relation to the former, most police officers in sex crime units viewed the courts as lacking efficacy in responding to sex crimes and punishing sex offenders:

Wesley: The only positive is that he's in jail, will be for a long time. Probably one of the biggest sentences we've ever got worked out in a plea deal, which was ten years and he'd already been in for two. So that's big in Canada, because we let everybody out. . . . Most guys are getting a year. Some are getting six months. And we're sending them right back out . . . based on maybe some conditions that a judge puts him on and says that he can't go on the Internet. . . . How do we know he's not back at home with his mom or his apartment by himself and in his bedroom he's got a laptop? . . . I mean, yes, they may be on the SOR [sex offender registry] and our SOR guy may visit his home and he may go in and make sure he doesn't have something once a year, but there's no provision in place where we have a SOR guy visiting him every single day, out of the blue, without a door knock. He's gotta announce himself. He's gotta request permission to go in. And if you're that deviant, all you gotta make sure is that laptop or that tablet isn't in plain view. Maybe it's tucked under a pillow. Maybe it's under a mattress.

Like a majority of the officers we interviewed, Wesley does not believe that the criminal justice system in Canada adequately punishes sex offenders for their crimes or prevents recidivism (n=45). This finding is consistent with the academic literature, which acknowledges the "tough on crime" attitudes among police officers (Blumenstein, Fridell, and Jones 2012; Fielding and Fielding 1991). Wesley is cynical about the effectiveness of the criminal justice system to monitor sex offenders and the efficacy of prisons to rehabilitate/treat sex offenders. He is convinced of their artifice in the face of being monitored; his cynicism toward the perpetrator of sex crimes underlies this distrust. Wesley questions the efficacy of the sex offender registry to manage and monitor sex offenders. The taint of the sex offender becomes intertwined with cynicism as it regards the efficacy of the criminal justice system.

On the other hand, cynicism is experienced in relation to the treatment of victims of sex crimes and the court process. Jordan (2001, 2008) explains that the criminal justice system and victims remain worlds apart in terms of their perspectives and needs. She points to reports of female sexual assault victims' experiences reporting to police and remaining largely unsatisfied with the end result. This lack of satisfaction is extended to the courts. When asked about the court process, a majority of interviewees indicate that the courts were at odds with the goals of police and victims. Consider the following two narratives:

Serena: I feel bad for victims. I always tell my victims that just because I've made an arrest and we've charged someone, you're not—I'm not guaranteeing closure for you. Because the court process revictimizes people. That's our justice system . . . that's how it works.

Miriam: I think it is re-victimizing victims almost every time. I don't know any investigator that's going to tell you they love the justice system in Canada. Like three years for a child to step foot in a court? People getting off on technicalities that have nothing to do with the offence. Expecting people to have such a vivid memory of an event and being able to tear them apart at the most minute of detail. . . . People say it all the time that the court protects the accused more than they protect the victim. Now I'm all for a fair trial, but I think the line has just been skewed, and there's certain amount of allowance and luxuries and concessions that—you're doing more than ensuring a fair trial here.

Although empathetic toward victims, Serena is cynical about how the justice system works. She recognizes that the purported end goal of the justice system is to produce some resolution, and while she holds offenders accountable, Serena views the courts as revictimizing victims as witnesses and failing to produce justice or protection. Miriam offers more insight as to how the system fails. She interprets the expectations of the court system on the victims—both in terms of memory and emotions—as an unreasonable burden on victims. According to Miriam and a number of other interviewees (n=40), the balance of justice is thought to be more in favor of the accused than the victim. Cynicism is directed at the disjuncture between the purported means and ends of the system. Such organizational cynicism involves a belief that the justice system lacks integrity and is not committed to fairness, honesty, and sincerity. The form of dirty work then involves not only managing their own cynicism but also dealing with more unpleasant interactions with victims at the worst moments of their lives.

DISCUSSION

A bind exists among police officers working in sex crime units. They are to manage morally tainted aspects of police work, and how they do so at times may leave their values compromised. The fact that perpetrators of sex crimes against women and children are viewed as depraved is long recognized (Lynch 2002). People involved in dirty work make sense of what they do in multiple ways (Hughes et al. 2017; Simpson et al. 2014; Meara 1974). We have argued that cynicism emerges in sex offense policing as a way of mitigating, normalizing, or neutralizing these experiences and emotions. Some officers report needing to act in ways that made them uncomfortable, even that compromise their values, to befriend and interact online with the accused to make him or her feel comfortable enough to provide the evidence necessary to lay charges and later secure a conviction. Not only does this evidence an operational cynicism, but such practices reveal a brewing self-directed cynicism and dissatisfaction with their own person (and thus occupation)—even though such acts are too often considered a "normal" part of their 'dirty' job.

The introduction of the internet and online social worlds complicates existing sex crimes and, in some cases, creates entirely new venues for sex crimes to take place (e.g., on the Dark Web), all which present serious challenges to police work. The dirty work of sex crime units, especially internet child exploitation units, falls outside the realm of traditional police work. As a consequence, many interviewees report feeling that their occupational work was first enveloped in an aura of mystique and then either unrecognized as "police work" or othered as "technological services." The pseudo alienation from other officers and traditional police work can impact police occupational satisfaction and result in both operational- and organizational-directed cynicism. The changing nature of police work (Sanders, Weston, and Schott 2015), which now includes technical supports and online investigation, requires greater recognition across police service organizations of all sizes to assist in reducing the cynicism police experience when working in some of the most trying fields of police work—which is only intensified when dealing with sex crime victims.

Too often police are working with individuals who must relive their most psychologically traumatizing life experience. Despite the hardship tied to such interrogations, varying degrees of cynicism directed toward victims remain; he or she who may constitute the "ideal" victim would be directed the least cynicism (Christie 1986). Future research is necessary to understand how victim characteristics can dictate, for certain sex crime investigators, the credibility and authenticity of those who claim the status of victim and how this is shaped within the context of sex crime investigation. Such realities can shape police work in sex crime units and hamper the police's ability to ensure a victim is not revictimized during investigative processes.

Officer cynicism is, then, shaped by their work role and environment. Both encourage a manifestation of cynicism that leaves all members of society positioned as potential sex offenders. This also extends beyond the confines of police occupational responsibilities and practices. Some officers express a need to self-regulate their own off duty actions to ensure their actions cannot be misconstrued as inappropriate, particularly sexually inappropriate toward a child. For this reason, we have claimed that cynicism in police dirty work is not only experienced in relation to "front" and "back" regions (Dick 2005) but also across multiple social dimensions. In this way, the police occupational environment for sex crime investigators reshapes the potentiality of all individuals who come into contact with the systems of justice, due to cynicism(s) that shapes their identity and interpretations.

Police officers working in sex crime units across Canada express multi-faceted forms of cynicism. These cynical attitudes are directed at multiple participants in the criminal justice system, including not only offenders and victims but also those with whom they interact in their personal lives. Cynicism is expressed as a product of dirty work and includes dealing with the courts, officers' too often perceived inability to achieve justice for victims, and attacks on officers' credibility and authenticity. Cynicism is also directed at those individuals and structures within or associated with the justice system. The latter reveals a form of organizational cynicism that renders the integrity of the criminal justice system fallible and under scrutiny. Future research on those tasked with carrying out dirty work associated with policing cyber environments should expand on the insights regarding cynicism offered here as a means for understanding the breadth of this experience. Future researchers should also consider how police cope with these negative aspects of dirty work and the cynicism associated with sex crime investigations, including the reliance on informal mechanisms like "gallows humour" (Ashforth et al. 2007, 163), drugs and alcohol, and formal resources such as psychological services.[1] Finally, research should explore burnout, career shifts, and dis-identification in sex crime units.

NOTE

1. For discussion of the coping strategies and organizational responses to cynicism and occupational stress among this cohort of participants, see Spencer, Dodge, Ricciardelli, and Ballucci (2021).

Chapter 7

Conclusion

In *Dirty Work*, Eyal Press (2021) documents the morally questionable forms of work that individuals, primarily of lesser socioeconomic status, perform on behalf of society. He examines the occupational hazards associated with purported morally questionable elements that "dirty" workers must engage with and the resulting stigma, shame, and moral injury that is endured given their occupational positioning. Press's contention is that dirty work has been offloaded onto low-income workers, undocumented immigrants, women, and racialized people.

The sex crime investigators featured throughout our book engage with dirty work, which forces them to engage with morally questionable materials and listen to the emotionally corrosive stories associated with sexual violence against children, youth, and adults. While sex crime investigators are, arguably, reasonably remunerated for their dirty work, the high level of taint attached to their work and lack of respect received from colleagues and societal members more broadly results in varying levels of psychological trauma that manifests in their day-to-day lives (see Spencer et al. 2021). Part of our approach to appreciative inquiry meant that we not only recognized the extreme difficulty of their work and the dedication with which they completed their occupational responsibilities (even those that were trying, difficult, and harmful) but also were deeply affected by hearing their stories and witnessing their psychological trauma. At times, we saw the destructive consequences on investigators of their dirty work. We interviewed participants with diagnosed posttraumatic stress disorder (PTSD) and others who left their occupation because of psychological trauma, and we also saw the hurt endured as officers took statements from victims and witnesses. We saw participants change in personality due to working in internet child exploitation units; we learned that one was never to listen and view videos of child victimization simultaneously because of the personal harm that likely would be an outcome; and we witnessed officers fall because of their work. Participants with compromised mental health and well-being were not rarities in our sample; unfortunately, it was all too common, and we, as researchers, learned to support each other as we heard rather trying stories but maintained participant confidentiality and anonymity.

Appreciative inquiry, as a criminological disposition, is arguably against the broader critical orientation that operates on the basis that there is nothing redeemable about police and the doxa that critical criminologists should always side with and be empathetic toward those subject to policing. This orientation, which we refer to as "critical," is only intensified within broader cultural movements—such as #defundthepolice—that call for the abolition of police and a reallocation of funds toward community organizations. Whereas we are sympathetic to individuals pointing to police abuses of racialized individuals and other groups, we view the dirty work that sex crime investigators, specifically, carry out as necessary. We view the police role in sexual victimization cases as necessary and providing a key function for the greater well-being of society and individuals, particularly those victimized. In addition, we assert that as the collective "we"—that is, society—we want "someone" to do something about such crimes, especially sexual violence against children. How to respond to the violence and harm perpetrated by assailants of sexual violence, however, does not come up in debates about police funding nor is it conceptualized, in the main, as police work. When sex crime investigators are featured in the media, be it social media, traditional newspapers, or film and television, they are cleansed of taint, and the organizational situatedness of sex crime units—regarded as, on the one hand, not "real" police work and, on the other hand, as suspect—is altogether ignored. As such, any sympathies for the women and men who make up sex crime units are absent, and as such, they do not receive the much-needed financial and organizational support necessary to effectively carry out their investigations in any sort of remedial way. We want to be clear that we are not saying societal members would be unsupportive of investing in limiting, ending, or responding to incidents of sexual violence. Instead, we are simply putting forth that discussions about "defunding" police often ignore the very real and constant realities in which police are operating, and these realities include sex crimes. Responding to sex crimes is, as one investigator explained to us, equivalent to emptying a tub with a tablespoon while the water continues to run. To this end, we appreciate that there are people—officers—willing to police these realities, to stop the making and distribution of child pornography, to categorize images of child pornography, to interrogate constitutions of consent, to respond to victims of rape or sexual violence, and to help and support child victims and the many others who suffer collateral consequences of sex crimes.

In our own individual ways, we were deeply affected by our submersion in the data collection for this book. While not blinded by over empathizing with our research subjects, we were and remain committed to recognizing the devastating impacts that such investigations have on the emotional and psychological well-being of investigators. In addition, we are forever affected by the stories presented and reflections offered by the officers we interviewed. Concomitantly, we recognize the limitations of our research and the necessity of future research, as well as possible ways sex crime investigators can improve their individual and organizational practices. In what follows, we reflect on the contributions of our research, future lines of inquiry, and recommendations in terms of changing police practices.

OVERVIEW

In our book, we show that how a nation, Canada, defines and structures its response to sex crime matters for the delivery of criminal justice. In addition, we detail how the emergence of digital infrastructures, or as we refer to them here, digital assemblages, have intersected with criminal law in ways that, to varying degrees, reflect the nature of sex crimes. We demonstrate that police officers feel they need more tools and training to effectively respond to the role that digital evidence increasingly plays in sex crimes. We show that the overwhelming societal changes brought on by the digital age have had specific impacts on the character of sex crime investigations and such reverberations need to be better understood and incorporated into policing and the criminal justice system more broadly.

We explored the barriers to police investigation and response to sexual violence and harassment, which include the changing nature of sexual violence and the significant budgetary constraints placed on police. Simultaneously, sexual violence and harassment are continuously evolving in modern society with innovations in digital communication technologies and the internet. In response, police face additional challenges that include remaining up to date on technology and social media and managing the quantity of digital evidence (photographs, videos, or social media logs) requiring assessment and categorization. Police must have training on and work to modernize the resources and facilities required to investigate technological or digital evidence. In addition, they must navigate the complexity of responding to a case that includes digital and in-person sexual violence elements (which may require cooperation between cybercrime or internet child exploitation units and sexual assault and child abuse units) and deal with cases that involve suspects offending via the internet who are located in different geographical areas than the complainant. They must comprehend the nature of harms caused by online sexual violence and responding to cases that rely on cooperation from foreign technology or social media companies.

We examined the seeming range of police interpretation of victims, from those whose victimization is perceived as obvious (e.g., undoubtedly a victim of a sex crime) to those whose victimization is perceived as more challenging to support professionally (e.g., a victim whose claims cannot be substantiated with evidence that surpasses the standard of reasonable doubt). We explored if and how perceptions of victims translate into police perceptions of their interactions with victims (e.g., how officers feel the victim can be treated) and their understandings of the possible outcomes that can be offered in the investigation (e.g., charges laid). We highlighted the impediments officers encounter as they strive to balance their occupational role with victim needs, always paying heed to the fact that officer dispositions impact how victims judge the justice meted out in the wake of their victimization.

We analyzed the networking of Canadian police agencies with governmental and nongovernmental organizations in response to child victims of sex crimes. We examined police understandings of collaboration as well as their expressed interpretations of collaborations' benefits and challenges. By focusing on police investigations and responses to child victims, specifically, and examining how police organizations negotiate their partnerships with community organizations, we reveal the often vague and fluctuating boundaries of roles and responsibilities between police and community partners. This fluctuation creates challenges and tension and, in some cases, can jeopardize the ability of police to successfully lay charges. Police also acknowledged the value of support provided to child victims and their families through productive community partnerships.

In the final empirical chapter, we examined the experiences and expressions of cynicism among Canadian police working in sex crime–related units. We confirm that officer cynicism is not exclusively directed at criminalized individuals. It encompasses the operational and organizational aspects of police work and seeps into officers' lived experiences outside of work. Due to their engagement in dirty work, sex crime investigators experience organizational and intraorganizational sources of cynicism in dealing with morally tainted forms of criminal offending. We analyzed sex crime unit members' sources of cynicism in relation to sex crimes and the digital world and explored sources of cynicism in police organizations as well as other branches of the criminal justice system. We demonstrate how cynicism seeps into relationships outside of the occupation. We show that cynicism related to police dirty work is experienced not only in relation to "front" and "back" regions but also in multiple organizational and social spheres. We addressed the implications of investigating and responding to sex crimes, the underexplored dirty work associated with policing digital environments, and the morally tainted elements of such policing tasks.

CONTRIBUTIONS AND RECOMMENDATIONS

By identifying the challenges and benefits of networked policing with regard to victim support, we contribute to Canadian criminological scholarship on networked policing in response to child sexual abuse in three key ways. First, by expanding analyses of networked policing from functions of governance and surveillance toward that of support for child victims of sex crimes, we offer a nuanced understanding of contemporary partnership practices. Second, by probing how traditional police roles and responsibilities are simultaneously entrenched and challenged through collaborative projects with child victim–oriented community partners, we reveal how police interpret the tensions and benefits that come with joint investigations and responses. Third, by examining how collaborative challenges are being addressed within Canada's relatively newly implemented child advocacy centers (CACs), we draw attention to CACs development in Canadian policing and identify some of the possibilities and challenges ahead.

Our work provides a foundation for further research on networked responses to child victims and sex crimes although with select limitations. First, respondents were all police officers, and as such, the perspective of community partner agencies, in terms of the benefits and challenges of partnerships, is notably absent. Second, we do not claim our findings are generalizable to all police services in Canada; rather, we suggest that qualitative findings such as these can elucidate contemporary Canadian policing practices with regard to manifold victims of sex crimes, and we provisionally offer insights to the problems and benefits associated with networked responses from the perspective of police.

Through our analyses, we provide qualitative insights into the networked role of police response to child victims of sex crimes and show that variance in the degree partnerships are formalized and co-located impacts police attitudes toward community partners and their willingness to share information. Police officers were much more likely to speak positively about the process of joint investigations and information sharing in organizations affiliated with established CACs. Collaborative tensions, such as differing mandates and blurred boundaries, were present in all research sites, but police working in and alongside advocacy centers were more likely to recognize that the safety and best interest of children were shared goals across all partner agencies. Several officers expressed the hope that more CACs will be established in Canada and that existing ones receive adequate funding to continue and to grow.[1] The challenges they identify, however, demonstrate that there is a need for clearly demarcated roles and an understanding of these varying but complementing roles if these partnerships are to be most successful.

We assert that specialized training in digital communication technologies, quick responses, and strategies for effective communication with victims and families, as well as police having more time for investigations by reducing caseloads, can all have a positive impact on the outcome of sex crime–related investigations. Specifically, to respond to the ever-changing technologies and growing number of cases with an online or digital element, there must be continuous training in technologies and more personnel dedicated to processing electronic evidence and assisting in the technological aspects of investigations. Moreover, training must be ongoing, focusing not only on the latest technologies but also on the latest in social media and other online spaces that can become the "space" of online or in-person sexual victimization. With technologies developing, crime—and thus policing—is changing in response; proactive policing is essential yet difficult given that police must prioritize responses to calls for service over proactive learning, development, and planning.

Online aspects of sex crimes defy municipal, provincial, and national boundaries—the internet is not constrained by geography. Interorganizational collaboration is necessary to address crime in this globalized environment where technology is changing faster than the resources available to police them. For example, interviewed police officers discussed how widespread the practice of sharing nude photos is among youth and, therefore, how broad education about sharing these images is needed rather than criminal responses in many cases.

The overwhelming majority of police officers who participated in our study confirmed the efficacy of CACs for producing positive outcomes during investigations into sexual violence perpetrated against children and youth and for reducing the trauma associated with navigating the criminal justice system. CACs can and do vary in form; there is not a one-size-fits-all solution. In terms of best practice, rural areas require a mobile unit, while urban centers should develop large multiorganizational centers. Most important, however, is the fact that CACs can and should create collaborations between police organizations, children's aid societies, medical services, and various other local support services (i.e., counseling, parenting classes, emergency room professionals).

Officers' mental health matters and has important implications for their continued operation in their roles and the quality of service provided to victims of sexual violence and harassment. As such, we advocate for education and training for officers regarding how to cope with the diverse forms of psychological trauma tied to their occupational role and experiences. Government action requires continued support for formal psychological services and the prioritization of informal support mechanisms to better serve police officers. The Ontario government recently announced a new strategy for public safety personnel who suffer from posttraumatic stress disorder (PTSD). According to the Canadian Mental Health Association (CMHA) (2016), PTSD is a psychological condition that develops from single or chronic exposure to psychologically traumatic events, including crimes, sexual abuse or violence, accidents, war, conflict, or other difficult situations (see also Ricciardelli et al. 2021). Given that police are responsible for law enforcement, peacekeeping, first responses, social well-being, and civilian safety (see Huey and Ricciardelli 2015), officers are inherently exposed to psychologically as well as physically traumatic events throughout their careers. These traumatic events can include, although not exclusively, responding to motor vehicle collisions, coping with a variety of potentially life-threatening or dangerous situations, dealing with individuals suffering from mental illness, or responding to sexual victimization. Police officers, and other public safety personnel like paramedics, nurses, public safety communicators, correctional workers, and firefighters, are at an increased risk of PTSD (Maran et al. 2015; Ménard and Arter 2013). Speaking in support of the new strategy, one officer in our study stated: "PTSD is at the forefront of first responders right now. I've seen 26 years of garbage" (Scott).

Indeed, Badge of Life Canada (BOLC), formerly led by retired police officer Bill Rusk, remains behind the Supporting Ontario's First Responders Act (2016). This act represents an effective first step toward addressing the stigma associated with mental health and ensuring medical resources are available for public safety personnel in the province of Ontario, Canada. In this section, we address some of the challenges related to mental health and how best practices around mental health and well-being can have a positive impact on police and the investigation of and response to sexual violence and harassment more broadly. Officers' mental health matters insofar as health has important implications that are not limited to officers' continued operation in their roles and the quality of service provided to victims of sex crimes. Police involved in sexual violence and harassment investigations are often exposed to a considerable amount of psychological trauma—including secondary or vicarious trauma—as they interview victims and accused individuals and view graphic and disturbing images and videos. Additionally, officers are often left concerned about the well-being of the victims they interview because charges are not laid in their case or because the victims seem to be coping poorly. Some officers in our sample spoke about colleagues in their unit who were off on leave because they experienced psychological trauma while on duty.

To facilitate greater use of mental health services, concerns regarding the confidentiality of formal mental health services must be addressed. One way to do so is for police organizations to develop partnerships with community agencies or, as evinced in select police services, to have mandated psychological visits and assessments for individuals working in such challenging environments (i.e., internet child exploitation officers or officers investigating particularly disturbing cases). Delivering formal psychological support from outside the police organization may ease concerns regarding the confidentiality of such interactions. Moreover, mandated psychological assessments may ease the stigma of seeking assistance if it is what police officers want (Newell et al. 2022). Maran and colleagues (2015) suggest that developing an educational component to train officers to identify and manage occupational stress can help avoid the development of chronic stress. Added to that, we also advocate for education and training for officers to deal with the diverse forms of psychological trauma that are tied to their occupational role and experiences, as well as the organizational stressors and other factors shaping occupational stress injuries or posttraumatic stress injuries. While the vast majority of officers were appreciative of expanded medical resources to address mental health needs, they still preferred to use informal responses when coping with psychological trauma. These informal responses include participating in peer support groups; engaging in informal conversations with peers, supervisors, and trusted loved ones; and living a healthy lifestyle, including healthy eating habits and exercise. For instance, Brian said, "Having the cup of coffee or door-to-door chats out in the world, they're more effective I think than formal routes." Government action, then, requires not only continued support for formal services but also a prioritization of informal support mechanisms to serve police officers; ideally, all such supports should be evidence informed and evaluated. Thus, this means a continuation of investment in and promotion of formal services to address mental health–related concerns among police—which translates into more funding for mental health services, not less.

NOTE

1. As successful as the model of CACs appears to be, they are currently limited to responding to crimes against children. Such a model of holistic, collaborative responses to adult sexual assault and domestic violence remains absent.

References

Aldrich, H., and D. Herker. 1977. "Boundary Spanning Roles and Organization Structure." *Academy of Management Review* 2 (2): 217–30.

Aries, P. 1965. *Centuries of Childhood: A Social History of Family Life*. New York: Vintage.

———. 2012. "The Discovery of Childhood." In *The Global History of Childhood Reader*, edited by H. Morrison, 1:9–20. London; New York: Routledge.

Arnes, A. 2018. *Digital Forensics*. Hoboken, NJ: Wiley.

Ashforth, B., and G. Kreiner. 1999. "'How Can You Do It?' Dirty Work and the Challenge of Constructing a Positive Identity." *Academy of Management Review* 24 (3): 413–34.

Ashforth, B., G. E. Kreiner, M. A. Clark, and M. Fugate. 2007. "Normalizing Dirty Work: Managerial Tactics for Countering Occupational Taint." *Academy of Management Journal* 50 (1): 149–74.

Bakker, A. B., and E. Heuven. 2006. "Emotional Dissonance, Burnout, and In-Role Performance among Nurses and Police Officers." *International Journal of Stress Management* 13 (4): 423–40.

Balch, R. 1972. "The Police Personality: Fact or Fiction?" *Journal of Criminal Law, Criminology, and Police Science* 63 (1): 106–19.

Baym, N. 2011. *Personal Connections in the Digital Age*. Cambridge: Polity.

BBC News. 2016. "Police Forces 'Overwhelmed' by Digital Evidence, Watchdog Finds." BBC News, November 3, 2016. https://www.bbc.com/news/uk-37846705.

Beckett, K., and N. Murakawa. 2012. "Mapping the Shadow Carceral State: Toward an Institutionally Capacious Approach to Punishment." *Theoretical Criminology* 16 (2): 221–44.

Beebe, N. 2009. "Digital Forensic Research: The Good, the Bad, and the Unaddressed." In *Advances in Digital Forensics*, edited by G. Peterson and S. Shenoi, 5:17–36. Berlin; Heidelberg: Springer.

Belknap, J. 2010. "Rape: Too Hard to Report and Too Easy to Discredit Victims." *Violence against Women* 16 (12): 1335–44.

Bennett, J. 2004. "The Force of Things: Steps toward an Ecology of Matter." *Political Theory* 32 (3): 347–72.

————. 2009. *Vibrant Matter: A Political Ecology of Things*. Durham, NC: Duke University Press.

Bennett, R., and E. Schmitt. 2002. "The Effect of Work Environment on Levels of Police Cynicism: A Comparative Study." *Police Quarterly* 5 (4): 492–522.

Benoit, C., L. Shumka, R. Phillips, M. C. Kennedy, and L. Belle-Isle. 2015. *Issue Brief: Sexual Violence against Women in Canada*. Ottawa: Federal-Provincial-Territorial Senior Officials for the Status of Women.

Best, J. 1987. "Rhetoric in Claims-Making: Constructing the Missing Children Problem." *Social Problems* 34 (2): 101–21.

Bidgoli, M., and J. Grossklags. 2016. "End User Cybercrime Reporting: What We Know and What We Can Do to Improve It." *IEEE Xplore*, November 17, 2016, 1–6.

Blakemore, B. 2012. "Cyberspace, Cyber Crime and Cyber Terrorism." In *Policing Cyber Hate, Cyber Threats and Cyber Terrorism*, edited by I. Awan and B. Blakemore, 5–20. Farnham, UK: Ashgate.

Bluett-Boyd, N., B. Fileborn, A. Quadara, and S. Moore. 2013. *The Role of Emerging Communication Technologies in Experiences of Sexual Violence: A New Legal Frontier?* Report 23. Melbourne: Australian Institute of Family Studies.

Blumenstein, L., L. Fridell, and S. Jones. 2012. "The Link between Traditional Police Subculture and Police Intimate Partner Violence." *Policing* 35 (1): 147–64.

Bowleg, L. 2012. "The Problem with the Phrase Women and Minorities: Intersectionality—an Important Theoretical Framework for Public Health." *American Journal of Public Health* 102 (7): 1267–73.

boyd, d. 2010. "Social Network Sites as Networked Publics: Affordances, Dynamics, and Implications." In *Networked Self: Identity, Community, and Culture on Social Network Sites*, edited by Zizi Papacharissi, 39–58. New York: Routledge.

Bradford, B., J. Jackson, and E. A. Stanko. 2009. "Contact and Confidence: Revisiting the Impact of Public Encounters with the Police." *Policing and Society* 19 (1): 20–46.

Brewer, R. 2013. "Enhancing Crime Control Partnerships across Government: Examining the Role of Trust and Social Capital on American and Australian Waterfronts." *Police Quarterly* 16 (4): 371–94.

Brown, G. P., J. P. Hirdes, and B. E. Fries. 2015. "Measuring the Prevalence of Current, Severe Symptoms of Mental Health Problems in a Canadian Correctional Population: Implications for Delivery of Mental Health Services for Inmates." *International Journal of Offender Therapy and Comparative Criminology* 59 (1): 27–50.

Brown, G. R. 2015. "The Blue Line on Thin Ice: Police Use of Force Modifications in the Era of Cameraphones and YouTube." *British Journal of Criminology* 56:293–312.

Brown, M. K. 1988. *Working the Street: Police Discretion and the Dilemmas of Reform*. New York: Russell Sage Foundation.

Bullock, K., N. Tilley, and R. Erol. 2006. *Problem-Oriented Policing and Partnerships: Implementing an Evidence-Based Approach to Crime Reduction*. Cullompton, UK: Willan.

Burke, R. J., and A. Mikkelsen. 2005a. "Career Stage and Police Cynicism." *Psychological Reports* 96 (3): 989–92.

———. 2005b. "Gender Issues in Policing: Do They Matter?" *Women in Management Review* 20 (2): 133–43.

Butt, D. 2017. "We Are Failing the Community of Sexual Assault Victims." *Globe and Mail*, February 4, 2017.

Campbell, B. A., T. A. Menaker, and W. R. King. 2015. "The Determination of Victim Credibility by Adult and Juvenile Sexual Assault Investigators." *Journal of Criminal Justice* 43 (1): 29–39.

Campbell, J. L., C. Quincy, J. Osserman, and O. K. Pedersen. 2013. "Coding In-Depth Semistructured Interviews: Problems of Unitization and Intercoder Reliability and Agreement." *Sociological Methods & Research* 42:294–320.

Campeau, H. 2015. "'Police Culture' at Work: Making Sense of Police Oversight." *British Journal of Criminology* 55 (4): 669–87.

Canadian Mental Health Association. 2016. "Post-traumatic Stress Disorder." CMHA, February 28, 2016. http://www.cmha.ca/mental_health/post-traumatic -stress-disorder/#.VxUIdoQ4mRs.

Caplan, J. 2003. "Police Cynicism: Police Survival Tool?" *Police Journal* 76 (4): 304–13.

Carbone-Lopez, K., L. A. Slocum, and C. Kruttschnitt. 2016. "'Police Wouldn't Give You No Help': Female Offenders on Reporting Sexual Assault to Police." *Violence against Women* 22 (3): 366–96.

Carey, J. W., M. Morgan, and M. J. Oxtoby. 1996. "Intercoder Agreement in Analysis of Responses to Open-Ended Interview Questions: Examples from Tuberculosis Research." *Field Methods* 8 (3): 1–5.

Carimico, G., T. Huynh, and S. Wells. 2016. "Rape and Sexual Assault." *Georgetown Journal of Gender and the Law* 17:359–410.

Carlan, P. E., and J. A. Lewis. 2009. "Dissecting Police Professionalism: A Comparison of Predictors within Five Professionalism Subsets." *Police Quarterly* 4:370–87.

Cartwright, S., and N. Holmes. 2006. "The Meaning of Work: The Challenge of Regaining Employee Engagement and Reducing Cynicism." *Human Resource Management Review* 16 (2): 199–208.

Casey, E. 2011. *Digital Evidence and Computer Crime: Forensic Science, Computers, and the Internet.* Cambridge: Academic Press.

Cashman, D. C. 2000. "Negotiating Gender: A Comparison of Rape Laws in Canada, Finland, and Pakistan." *Dalhousie Journal of Legal Studies* 9:120–87.

Chaikin, D. 2006. "Network Investigations of Cyber Attacks: The Limits of Digital Evidence." *Crime, Law & Social Change* 46:239–56.

Chan, J. B. L. 1996. "Changing Police Culture." *British Journal of Criminology* 36 (1): 109–34.

———. 1997. *Changing Police Culture: Policing in a Multicultural Society.* Cambridge: Cambridge University Press.

————. 2007. "Police Stress and Occupational Culture." In *Police Occupational Culture*, edited by M. O'Neill, M. Marks, and A. Singh, 129–51. Bingley, UK: Emerald.

Chan, J. B. L., C. Devery, and S. Doran. 2003. *Fair Cop: Learning the Art of Policing.* Toronto: University of Toronto Press.

Charmaz, K. 2006. *Constructing Grounded Theory: A Practical Guide through Qualitative Analysis.* 1st ed. London; Thousand Oaks, CA: Sage.

Chesney-Lind, M. 2002. "Criminalizing Victimization: The Unintended Consequences of Pro-arrest Policies for Girls and Women." *Criminology & Public Policy* 2 (1): 81–90.

Child and Family Services Act. 2007. Ontario.

Child, Youth and Family Enhancement Act. 2000. Alberta.

Chon, D. S., and J. E. Clifford. 2021. "The Impacts of International Rape Laws upon Official Rape Rates." *International Journal of Offender Therapy and Comparative Criminology* 65:244–60.

Christie, N. 1986. "An Ideal Victim." In *From Crime Policy to Victim Policy: Reinventing the Justice System*, edited by E. A. Fattah, 17–30. London: Macmillan.

Clifford, R. D., ed. 2006. *Cybercrime: The Investigation, Prosecution, and Defense of a Computer-Related Crime.* 2nd ed. Durham, NC: Carolina Academic Press.

Cohen, S. 1985. *Visions of Social Control.* Cambridge: Polity.

Cole, S. A., and M. Lynch. 2006. "The Social and Legal Construction of Suspects." *Annual Review of Law and Social Science* 2:39–60.

Collins, C. S., and C. M. Stockton. 2018. "The Central Role of Theory in Qualitative Research." *International Journal of Qualitative Methods* 17 (1). https://doi.org/10.1177/1609406918797475.

Corbin, J., and A. Strauss. 2007. *Basics of Qualitative Research: Techniques and Procedures for Developing Grounded Theory.* 3rd ed. Thousand Oaks, CA: Sage.

Corrigan, R. 2013. "The New Trial by Ordeal: Rape Kits, Police Practices, and the Unintended Effects of Policy Innovation." *Law & Social Inquiry* 38 (4): 920–49.

Corsianos, M. 2009. *Policing and Gendered Justice: Examining the Possibilities.* Toronto: University of Toronto Press.

Crank, J. P. 1998. "Celebrating Agency Culture: Engaging a Traditional Cop's Heart in Organizational Change." In *Community Policing in a Rural Setting*, edited by Q. C. Thurman and E. McGarrell, 49–57. Cincinnati, OH: Anderson.

————. 2014. *Understanding Police Culture.* New York: Routledge.

Crank, J. P., R. G. Culbertson, E. D. Poole, and R. M. Regoli. 1987. "Measurement of Cynicism among Police Chiefs." *Journal of Criminal Justice* 15 (1): 37–48.

Crawford, A. 1997. *The Local Governance of Crime: Appeals to Community and Partnerships.* Oxford: Clarendon.

————. 2006. "Networked Governance and the Post-regulatory State? Steering, Rowing and Anchoring the Provision of Policing and Security." *Theoretical Criminology* 10 (4): 449–79.

Crenshaw, K. 1991. "Mapping the Margins: Intersectionality, Identity Politics, and Violence against Women of Color." *Stanford Law Review* 43 (6): 1241–99.

Creswell, J. 2012. *Qualitative Inquiry and Research Design.* 3rd ed. Los Angeles, CA: Sage.

Crimes Act. 1900, No. 40 (NSW).

Criminal Code of Canada. RSC 1985, c. C - 46.

Cronch, L. E., J. L. Viljoen, and D. J. Hansen. 2006. "Forensic Interviewing in Child Sexual Abuse Cases: Current Techniques and Future Directions." *Aggression and Violent Behavior* 11 (3): 195–207.

Cross, T. P., D. Finkelhor, and R. Ormrod. 2005. "Police Involvement in Child Protective Services Investigations: Literature Review and Secondary Data Analysis." *Child Maltreatment* 10 (3): 224–44.

Cross, T. P., L. M. Jones, W. A. Walsh, M. Simone, and D. Kolko. 2007. "Child Forensic Interviewing in Children's Advocacy Centers: Empirical Data on a Practice Model." *Child Abuse & Neglect* 31 (10): 1031–52.

Daly, K., and B. Bouhours. 2010. "Rape and Attrition in the Legal Process: A Comparative Analysis of Five Countries." *Crime and Justice* 39 (1): 565–650.

Davies, P., P. Francis, and C. Greer, eds. 2007. *Victims, Crime and Society.* London: Sage.

Dean, J., P. Brandes, and R. Dharwadkar. 1998. "Organizational Cynicism." *Academy of Management Review* 23 (2): 341–52.

Dean, M. 2010. *Governmentality: Power and Rule in Modern Society.* 2nd ed. London: Sage.

DeGaine, J. J. 2013. "Digital Evidence." *Army Lawyer* 7:7–34.

DeJong, C., A. Burgess-Proctor, and L. Elis. 2008. "Police Officer Perceptions of Intimate Partner Violence: An Analysis of Observational Data." *Violence and Victims* 23 (6): 683–97.

Department of Justice. 2016. *Child Advocacy Centres Initiative.* Washington, DC: DOJ.

Dick, P. 2005. "Dirty Work Designations: How Police Officers Account for Their Use of Coercive Force." *Human Relations* 58 (11): 63–90.

Diss, L. 2013. "Whether You 'Like' It or Not: The Inclusion of Social Media Evidence in Sexual Harassment Cases and How Courts Can Effectively Control It." *Boston College Law Review* 54 (4): 1841–80.

Dodge, A., D. Spencer, R. Ricciardelli, and D. Ballucci. 2019. "'This Isn't Your Father's Police Force': Digital Evidence in Sexual Assault Investigations." *Australian and New Zealand Journal of Criminology* 52 (4): 499–515.

Doolittle, R. 2017. "Why Police Dismiss 1 in 5 Sexual Assault Claims as Baseless." *Globe and Mail*, February 3, 2017.

Dorsey, R., and D. Giacopassi. 1986. "Assessing Gender Differences in the Levels of Cynicism among Police Officers." *American Journal of Police* 5:91–112.

Drew, S., M. Mills, and B. Gassaway, eds. 2007. *Dirty Work: The Social Construction of Taint.* Waco, TX: Baylor University Press.

Dunn, J. L. 2010. *Judging Victims: Why We Stigmatize Survivors, and How They Reclaim Respect.* Boulder, CO: Lynne Rienner.

Ebbe, O. N. I. 2013. "The Purpose of Comparative and International Criminal Justice Systems." In *Comparative and International Criminal Justice Systems: Policing,*

Judiciary, and Corrections, 3rd ed., edited by O. N. I. Ebbe, 3–8. Boca Raton, FL: CRC Press.

Edge, J., P. Buffington, and D. Slemons. 1980. "Anxiety and Cynicism: Companions of the Police Officer." *American Journal of Criminal Justice* 5 (2): 18–24.

Elias, R. 1986. *The Politics of Victimization: Victims, Victimology, and Human Rights.* Oxford: Oxford University Press.

Enciso, G., J. Maskaly, and C. Donner. 2017. "Organizational Cynicism in Policing: Examining the Development and Growth of Cynicism among New Police Recruits." *Policing* 40 (1): 86–98.

Faith, T., and C. Bekir. 2015. "Police Use of Technology to Fight against Crime." *European Scientific Journal* 11 (10): 286–96.

Faller, K. C., and J. Henry. 2000. "Child Sexual Abuse: A Case Study in Community Collaboration." *Child Abuse & Neglect* 24 (9): 1215–25.

Farkas, M. A., and P. K. Manning. 1997. "The Occupational Culture of Corrections and Police Officers." *Journal of Crime and Justice* 20 (2): 51–68.

Feenberg, A. 2002. *Transforming Technology: A Critical Theory Revisited.* Oxford: Oxford University Press.

Fielding, N. G., and J. Fielding. 1991. "Police Attitudes to Crime and Punishment: Certainties and Dilemmas." *British Journal of Criminology* 31 (1): 39–53.

Finkelhor, D., J. Wolak, and L. Berliner. 2001. "Police Reporting and Professional Help Seeking for Child Crime Victims: A Review." *Child Maltreatment* 6 (1): 17–30.

Finley, L. M. 1989. "Breaking Women's Silence in Law: The Dilemma of the Gendered Nature of Legal Reasoning Symposium: The Moral Lawyer." *Notre Dame Law Review* 64:886–910.

Flick, U. 2014. *An Introduction to Qualitative Research.* 5th ed. Thousand Oaks, CA: Sage.

Flyvbjerg, B. 2001. *Making Social Science Matter: Why Social Inquiry Fails and How It Can Succeed Again.* Cambridge: Cambridge University Press.

Frank, D. J., B. J. Camp, and S. A. Boutcher. 2010. "Worldwide Trends in the Criminal Regulation of Sex, 1945 to 2005." *American Sociological Review* 75 (6): 867–93.

Frank, D. J., T. Hardinge, and K. Wosick-Correa. 2009. "The Global Dimensions of Rape-Law Reform: A Cross-National Study of Policy Outcomes." *American Sociological Review* 74 (2): 272–90.

Gamache, D. 2012. "From Victim Safety to Victim Engagement: Comments on 'The Impact of Victim-Focused Outreach on Criminal Legal System Outcomes Following Police-Reported Intimate Partner Abuse.'" *Violence against Women* 18 (8): 882–88.

Garland, D. 1996. "The Limits of the Sovereign State: Strategies of Crime Control in Contemporary Society." *British Journal of Criminology* 36 (4): 445–71.

———. 2001. *The Culture of Control: Crime and Social Order in Contemporary Society.* Oxford: Oxford University Press.

Giacomantonio, C. 2014. "A Typology of Police Organizational Boundaries." *Policing and Society* 24 (5): 545–65.

Giordano, S. M. 2004. "Electronic Evidence and the Law." *Information Systems Frontiers* 6 (2): 161–74.

Goffman, E. 1963. *Stigma: Notes on the Management of Spoiled Identity*. London: Penguin.

Gogolin, G. 2010. "The Digital Crime Tsunami." *Digital Investigation* 7:3–8.

Goldsmith, A. 1990. "Taking Police Culture Seriously: Police Discretion and the Limits of Law." *Policing and Society* 1 (2): 91–114.

Goodison, S. E., R. C. Davis, and B. A. Jackson. 2015. *Digital Evidence and the US Criminal Justice System*. Santa Monica, CA: RAND Corp.

Gottehrer, G. 2015. "Connected Discovery: What the Ubiquity of Digital Evidence Means for Lawyers and Litigation." *Richmond Journal of Law & Technology* 22 (3): 1–27.

Government of Canada. Protecting Canadians from Online Crime Act. *R.S., c. C-46*. https://laws-lois.justice.gc.ca/eng/annualstatutes/2014_31/.

Grace, A., R. Ricciardelli, D. Spencer, and D. Ballucci. 2019. "Collaborative Policing: Networked Responses to Child Victims of Sex Crimes." *Child Abuse & Neglect* 93:197–207.

Graham, R. 2006. "Male Rape and the Careful Construction of the Male Victim." *Social & Legal Studies* 15 (2): 187–208.

Graves, W. 1996. "Police Cynicism: Causes and Cures." *FBI Law Enforcement Bulletin* 65 (6): 16–20.

Gregory, J., and S. Lees. 1999. *Policing Sexual Assault*. London: Routledge.

Haggerty, K. D., and R. V. Ericson. 2000. "The Surveillant Assemblage." *British Journal of Sociology* 51 (4): 605–22.

Hall, S. 1986. "On Postmodernism and Articulation: An Interview with Stuart Hall." *Journal of Communication Inquiry* 10 (2): 45–60.

Hallsworth, S., and J. Lea. 2011. "Reconstructing Leviathan: Emerging Contours of the Security State." *Theoretical Criminology* 15 (2): 141–57.

Hammond, S. A. 1998. *The Thin Book of Appreciative Inquiry*. 2nd ed. Bend: Thin Book.

Harkin, D., C. Whelan, and L. Chang. 2018. "The Challenges Facing Specialist Police Cyber-Crime Units: An Empirical Analysis." *Police Practice and Research* 19 (6): 519–36.

Heidegger, M. 1977. *The Question concerning Technology, and Other Essays*. New York: Garland.

Henry, N., and Powell, A. 2015. "Embodied Harms: Gender, Shame, and Technology-Facilitated Sexual Violence." *Violence against Women* 21 (6): 758–79. https://doi.org/10.1177/1077801215576581.

Herbert, J. L., and L. Bromfield. 2016. "Evidence for the Efficacy of the Child Advocacy Center Model: A Systematic Review." *Trauma, Violence, & Abuse* 17 (3): 341–57.

Heywood, C. 2001. *A History of Childhood: Children and Childhood in the West from Medieval to Modern Times*. 1st ed. London: Polity.

Hornor, G. 2008. "Child Advocacy Centers: Providing Support to Primary Care Providers." *Journal of Pediatric Health Care* 22 (1): 35–39.

Horsman, G. 2017. "Can We Continue to Effectively Police Digital Crime?" *Science and Justice* 57:448–54.

Howard, P. 2003. "Embedded Media: Who We Know, What We Know, and Society Online." In *Society Online: The Internet in Context*, edited by P. Howard and S. Jones, 1–27. Thousand Oaks, CA: Sage.

Hubel, G. S., C. Campbell, T. West, S. Friedenberg, A. Schreier, M. F. Flood, and D. J. Hansen. 2014. "Child Advocacy Center-Based Group Treatment for Child Sexual Abuse." *Journal of Child Sexual Abuse* 23 (3): 304–25.

Huey, L., and R. Broll. 2015. "'I Don't Find It Sexy at All': Criminal Investigators' Views of Media Glamorization of Police 'Dirty Work.'" *Policing and Society* 25 (2): 236–47.

Huey, L., and R. Ricciardelli. 2015. "'This Isn't What I Signed Up For' When Police Officer Role Expectations Conflict with the Realities of General Duty Police Work in Remote Communities." *International Journal of Police Science & Management* 17 (3): 194–203.

Hughes, E. 1962. "Good People and Dirty Work." *Social Problems* 10 (1): 3–11.

Hughes, J., R. Simpson, N. Slutskaya, A. Simpson, and K. Hughes. 2017. "Beyond the Symbolic: A Relational Approach to Dirty Work through a Study of Refuse Collectors and Street Cleaners." *Work, Employment and Society* 31 (1): 106–22.

Innes, M. 2003. *Investigating Murder: Detective Work and the Police Response to Criminal Homicide.* Oxford: Oxford University Press.

Irons, A., and H. Lallie. 2014. "Digital Forensics to Intelligent Forensics." *Future Internet* 6 (3): 584–96.

Jakobsson, N., and A. Kotsadam. 2011. "The Law and Economics of International Sex Slavery: Prostitution Laws and Trafficking for Sexual Exploitation." *European Journal of Law and Economics* 35 (1): 87–107.

Javaid, A. 2015. "Police Responses to, and Attitudes towards, Male Rape: Issues and Concerns." *International Journal of Police Science & Management* 17 (2): 81–90.

———. 2017. "Giving a Voice to the Voiceless: Police Responses to Male Rape." *Policing: A Journal of Policy and Practice* 11 (2): 146–56.

———. 2020. "The Unheard Victims: Gender, Policing and Sexual Violence." *Policing and Society* 30 (4): 412–28.

Jewkes, Y. 2013. "Public Policing and Internet Crime." In *Handbook of Internet Crime*, edited by Y. Jewkes and M. Yar, 525–45. New York: Routledge.

Joh, E. 2009. "Breaking the Law to Enforce It: Undercover Police Participation in Crime." *Stanford Law Review* 62 (1): 155–98.

Johnson, H. 2015. *Improving the Police Response to Crimes of Violence against Women: Ottawa Women Have Their Say.* Ottawa: University of Ottawa.

Jones, L. M., T. P. Cross, W. A. Walsh, and M. Simone. 2007. "Do Children's Advocacy Centers Improve Families' Experiences of Child Sexual Abuse Investigations?" *Child Abuse & Neglect* 31 (10): 1069–85.

Jordan, J. 2001. "Worlds Apart? Women, Rape and the Police Reporting Process." *British Journal of Criminology* 41 (4): 679–706.

———. 2008. "Perfect Victims, Perfect Policing? Improving Rape Complainants' Experiences of Police Investigations." *Public Administration* 86 (3): 699–719.

Kerr, O. 2005. "Digital Evidence and the New Criminal Procedure." *Columbia Law Review* 105 (1): 279–318.

Kilty, J., and S. Fabian. 2010. "Deconstructing an Invisible Identity: The Reena Virk Case." In *Reena Virk: Critical Perspectives on a Canadian Murder*, edited by M. Rajiva and S. Batacharya, 122–55. Toronto: Canadian Scholars' Press.

Kingston Frontenac Anti-violence Coordinating Committee. 2009. "A Coordinated Response to Child Abuse Investigative, Justice and Community Services for the City of Kingston and Frontenac County." https://kfacc.org/about-us/what-we-do/.

Koster, N.-S. N., K. F. Kuijpers, M. J. J. Kunst, and J. P. V. der Leun. 2016. "Crime Victims Perceptions of Police Behavior, Legitimacy, and Cooperation: A Review of the Literature." *Victims & Offenders* 11 (3): 392–435.

Kraftl, P. 2008. "Young People, Hope and Childhood-Hope." *Space and Culture* 11 (2): 81–92.

Kreiner, G., B. Ashforth, and D. Sluss. 2006. "Identity Dynamics in Occupational Dirty Work: Integrating Social Identity and System Justification Perspectives." *Organization Science* 17 (5): 619–36.

Kurasaki, K. 2000. "Intercoder Reliability for Validating Conclusions Drawn from Open-Ended Interview Data." *Field Methods* 12 (3): 179–94.

Kvale, S., and S. Brinkmann. 2008. *InterViews: Learning the Craft of Qualitative Research Interviewing*. 2nd ed. Thousand Oaks, CA: Sage.

Latour, B. 1999. *Pandora's Hope: Essays on the Reality of Science Studies*. Cambridge, MA: Harvard University Press.

———. 2004. *Politics of Nature: How to Bring the Sciences into Democracy*. 1st ed. Translated by C. Porter. Cambridge: Harvard University Press.

———. 2012. *We Have Never Been Modern*. Cambridge, MA: Harvard University Press.

Liebling, A. 1999. "Doing Research in Prison: Breaking the Silence?" *Theoretical Criminology* 3 (2): 147–73.

———. 2001. "Whose Side Are We On? Theory, Practice and Allegiances in Prisons Research." *British Journal of Criminology* 41 (3): 472–84.

Liebling, A., D. Price, and C. Elliott. 1999. "Appreciative Inquiry and Relationships in Prison." *Punishment & Society* 1 (1): 71–98.

Light, L., and G. Ruebsaat. 2006. *Police Classification of Sexual Assault Cases as Unfounded: An Exploratory Study*, 3–16. Ottawa: Department of Justice Canada.

Lingwood, J., L. L. Smith, and J. W. Bond. 2015. "Amateur versus Professional: Does the Recovery of Forensic Evidence Differ Depending on Who Assesses the Crime Scene?" *International Journal of Police Science & Management* 17 (1): 3–8.

Lloyd, S., and M. Burman. 1996. "Specialist Police Units and the Joint Investigation of Child Abuse." *Child Abuse Review* 5 (1): 4–15.

Loader, I. 2000. "Plural Policing and Democratic Governance." *Social & Legal Studies* 9 (3): 323–45.

Loftus, B. 2008. "Dominant Culture Interrupted: Recognition, Resentment and the Politics of Change in an English Police Force." *British Journal of Criminology* 48 (6): 756–77.

———. 2010. "Police Occupational Culture: Classic Themes, Altered Times." *Policing and Society* 20 (1): 1–20.

London Police Service and Children's Aid Society. 2002. "Protocol between the London Police Service and the Children's Aid Society of London and Middlesex." https://wayback.archive-it.org/16312/20211208221415/https://www .attorneygeneral.jus.gov.on.ca/inquiries/cornwall/en/hearings/exhibits/John_Liston /pdf/London_Protocol.pdf.

Losavio, M., K. C. Seigfried-Spellar, and J. J. Sloan. 2016. "Why Digital Forensics Is Not a Profession and How It Can Become One." *Criminal Justice Studies* 29 (2): 143–62.

Lotz, R., and R. Regoli. 1977. "Police Cynicism and Professionalism." *Human Relations* 30 (2): 175–86.

Lumsden, K. 2016. "Police Officer and Civilian Staff Receptivity to Research and Evidence-Based Policing in the UK: Providing a Contextual Understanding through Qualitative Interviews." *Policing: A Journal of Policy and Practice* 11 (2): 157–67.

Lynch, M. 2002. "Pedophiles and Cyber-predators as Contaminating Forces: The Language of Disgust, Pollution, and Boundary Invasions in Federal Debates on Sex Offender Legislation." *Law & Social Inquiry* 27 (3): 529–66.

MacVean, A., and C. Cox. 2012. "Police Education in a University Setting: Emerging Cultures and Attitudes." *Policing: A Journal of Policy and Practice* 6 (1): 16–25.

Maier, S. L. 2008. "I Have Heard Horrible Stories . . . Rape Victim Advocates' Perceptions of the Revictimization of Rape Victims by the Police and Medical System." *Violence against Women* 14 (7): 786–808.

———. 2014. *Rape, Victims, and Investigations: Experiences and Perceptions of Law Enforcement Officers Responding to Reported Rapes.* New York: Routledge.

Manning, P. K. 1977. *Police Work: The Social Organization of Policing.* Cambridge, MA: MIT Press.

———. 2007. "A Dialectic of Organisational and Occupational Culture." In *Police Occupational Culture*, edited by M. O'Neill, M. Marks, and A.-M. Singh, 8:47–83. Bingley, UK: Emerald.

———. 2008. *The Technology of Policing: Crime Mapping, Information Technology, and the Rationality of Crime Control.* New York: New York University Press.

Maran, A., A. Varetto, M. Zedda, and V. Ieraci. 2015. "Occupational Stress, Anxiety and Coping Strategies in Police Officers." *Occupational Medicine* 65 (6): 466–73.

Marshall, C., and G. B. Rossman. 2011. *Designing Qualitative Research.* 5th ed. Thousand Oaks, CA: Sage.

Martin, J. T. 2018. "Police and Policing." *Annual Review of Anthropology* 47 (1): 133–48.

Martin, P. Y. 2005. *Rape Work: Victims, Gender, and Emotions in Organization and Community Context.* New York: Routledge.

Maslach, C., S. E. Jackson, and M. Leiter. 1996. *Maslach Burnout Inventory: Manual.* 3rd ed. Palo Alto, CA: Consulting Psychologists Press.

McAra, L., and S. Mcvie. 2005. "The Usual Suspects? Street-Life, Young People and the Police." *Criminal Justice* 5 (1): 5–36.

McCarthy, D. J. 2013. "Gendering 'Soft' Policing: Multi-agency Working, Female Cops, and the Fluidities of Police Culture." *Policing and Society* 23 (2): 261–78.

McGarry, R., and S. Walklate. 2015. *Victims: Trauma, Testimony and Justice.* New York; London: Routledge.

McMahon-Howard, J. 2011. "Does the Controversy Matter? Comparing the Causal Determinants of the Adoption of Controversial and Noncontroversial Rape Law Reforms." *Law and Society Review* 45 (2): 401–35.

McMillan, L. 2018. "Police Officers' Perceptions of False Allegations of Rape." *Journal of Gender Studies* 27 (1): 9–21.

Meara, H. 1974. "Honor in Dirty Work: The Case of American Meat Cutters and Turkish Butchers." *Sociology of Work and Occupations* 1 (3): 259–83.

Ménard, K., and M. Arter. 2013. "Police Officer Alcohol Use and Trauma Symptoms: Associations with Critical Incidents, Coping, and Social Stressors." *International Journal of Stress Management* 20 (1): 37–56.

Miles, M. B., M. Huberman, and J. Saldana. 2013. *Qualitative Data Analysis.* 3rd ed. Thousand Oaks, CA: Sage.

Moran-Elis, J., and N. Fielding. 1996. "A National Survey of the Investigation of Child Sexual Abuse." *British Journal of Social Work* 26:337–56.

Mulla, S. 2014. *The Violence of Care: Rape Victims, Forensic Nurses, and Sexual Assault Intervention.* New York: New York University Press.

Murphy, K. 2015. "Does Procedural Justice Matter to Youth? Comparing Adults' and Youths' Willingness to Collaborate with Police." *Policing and Society* 25 (1): 53–76.

Newell, C. J., R. Ricciardelli, S. M. Czarnuch, and K. Martin. 2022. "Police Staff and Mental Health: Barriers and Recommendations for Improving Help-Seeking." *Police Practice and Research* 23 (1): 111–24.

Newman, B. S., and P. L. Dannenfesler. 2005. "Children's Protective Services and Law Enforcement: Fostering Partnerships in Investigations of Child Abuse." *Journal of Child Sexual Abuse* 14 (2): 97–111.

Niederhoffer, A. 1967. *Behind the Shield.* Garden City, NY: Doubleday.

Norton, R., and T. Grant. 2008. "Rape Myth in True and False Rape Allegations." *Psychology, Crime & Law* 14 (4): 275–85.

O'Connell, B. J., H. Holzman, and B. Armandi. 1986. "Police Cynicism and the Modes of Adaptation." *Journal of Police Science and Administration* 14:307–13.

O'Neill, M., and D. McCarthy. 2014. "(Re)Negotiating Police Culture through Partnership Working: Trust, Compromise and the 'New' Pragmatism." *Criminology and Criminal Justice* 14 (2): 143–59.

Page, A. D. 2007. "Behind the Blue Line: Investigating Police Officers' Attitudes toward Rape." *Journal of Police and Criminal Psychology* 22 (1): 22–32.

Palmer, G. 2001. *A Road Map for Digital Forensic Research.* Rome, NY: Air Force Research Laboratory.

Paoline, E. A., III. 2003. "Taking Stock: Toward a Richer Understanding of Police Culture." *Journal of Criminal Justice* 31 (3): 199–214.

Paoline, E. A., III, S. Meyers, and R. Worden. 2000. "Police Culture, Individualism, and Community Policing Evidence from Two Police Departments." *Justice Quarterly* 4 (3): 575–605.

Paoline, E. A., III, W. Terrill, and M. T. Rossler. 2015. "Higher Education, College Degree Major, and Police Occupational Attitudes." *Journal of Criminal Justice Education* 1:49–73.

Patton, M. 2001. *Qualitative Research and Evaluation Methods*. 3rd ed. Thousand Oaks, CA: Sage.

Perrin, B. 2017. *Victim Law: The Law of Victims of Crime in Canada*. Toronto: Carswell.

Phillips, R., C. Benoit, H. Hallgrimsdottir, and K. Vallance. 2012. "Courtesy Stigma: A Hidden Health Concern among Front-Line Service Providers to Sex Workers." *Sociology of Health and Illness* 34 (5): 681–96.

Pogrebin, M. R., and E. Poole. 1993. "Vice Isn't Nice: A Look at the Effects of Working Undercover." *Journal of Criminal Justice* 21 (4): 383–94.

Powell, A. 2010. "Configuring Consent: Emerging Technologies, Unauthorized Sexual Images and Sexual Assault." *Australian and New Zealand Journal of Criminology* 43: 76–90.

———. 2015. "Seeking Rape Justice: Formal and Informal Responses to Sexual Violence through Technosocial Counter-Publics." *Theoretical Criminology* 19 (4): 571–88.

Powell, A., and N. Henry. 2018. "Policing Technology-Facilitated Sexual Violence against Adult Victims: Police and Service Sector Perspectives." *Policing and Society* 28(3): 291–307.

Powell, A., G. Stratton, and R. Cameron. 2018. *Digital Criminology*. New York: Routledge.

Powell, M. B., P. Cassematis, M. Benson, S. Smallbone, and R. Wortley. 2014a. "Police Officers' Perceptions of the Challenges Involved in Internet Child Exploitation Investigation." *Policing* 37(3): 543–57.

———. 2014b. "Police Officers' Perceptions of Their Reactions to Viewing Internet Child Exploitation Material." *Journal of Police and Criminal Psychology* 30 (2): 103–11.

———. 2014c. "Police Officers' Strategies for Coping with the Stress of Investigating Internet Child Exploitation." *Traumatology* 20 (1): 32–42.

Press, E. 2021. *Dirty Work: Essential Jobs and the Hidden Toll of Inequality in America*. Illustrated ed. New York: Farrar, Straus & Giroux.

Prokos, A., and I. Padavic. 2002. "There Oughtta Be a Law against Bitches: Masculinity Lessons in Police Academy Training." *Gender, Work & Organization* 9 (4): 439–59.

Public Health Agency of Canada. 2008. *Canadian Incidence Study of Reported Child Abuse and Neglect—2008*. Ottawa: PHAC.

Rabe-Hemp, C. E. 2009. "POLICEwomen or PoliceWOMEN? Doing Gender and Police Work." *Feminist Criminology* 4 (2): 114–29.

Randall, M. 2010. "Sexual Assault Law, Credibility, and 'Ideal Victims': Consent, Resistance, and Victim Blaming." *Canadian Journal of Women and the Law* 22 (2): 397–433.

Regoli, R., J. Crank, and G. Rivera. 1990. "The Construction and Implementation of an Alternative Measure of Police Cynicism." *Criminal Justice and Behavior* 17 (4): 395–409.

Reiner, R. 2000. *The Politics of the Police*. 3rd ed. Oxford: Oxford University Press.

———. 2010. *The Politics of the Police*. 4th ed. Oxford: Oxford University Press.

Reuss-Ianni, E. 2011. *Two Cultures of Policing: Street Cops and Management Cops*. New Brunswick, NJ: Transaction.

Ricciardelli, R., S. Bornstein, A. Hall, and R. N. Carleton, eds. 2021. *Handbook of Posttraumatic Stress: Psychosocial, Cultural, and Biological Perspectives*. 1st ed. New York: Routledge.

Ricciardelli, R., and M. Moir. 2013. "Stigmatized among the Stigmatized: Sex Offenders in Canadian Penitentiaries." *Canadian Journal of Criminology and Criminal Justice* 55 (3): 353–85.

Ricciardelli, R., and D. C. Spencer. 2017. *Violence, Sex Offenders and Corrections*. New York: Routledge.

Rose, N. 1996. "The Death of the Social? Re-figuring the Territory of Government." *Economy and Society* 25 (3): 327–56.

———. 2000. "Government and Control." *British Journal of Criminology* 40:321–39.

Roulston, K. 2010. "Considering Quality in Qualitative Interviewing." *Qualitative Research* 10 (2): 199–228.

Sanders, C., C. Weston, and N. Schott. 2015. "Police Innovations, 'Secret Squirrels' and Accountability: Empirically Examining the Integration of Intelligence-Led Policing in Canada." *British Journal of Criminology* 55 (4): 711–29.

Scanlan, D. 2011. *Digital Evidence in Criminal Law*. Aurora: Thomson Reuters.

Schaufeli, W. B., and D. Enzmann. 1998. *The Burnout Companion to Study and Practice: A Critical Analysis*. Washington, DC: Taylor & Francis.

Sedlak, A. J., D. Schultz, S. J. Wells, P. Lyons, H. J. Doueck, and F. Gragg. 2006. "Child Protection and Justice Systems Processing of Serious Child Abuse and Neglect Cases." *Child Abuse & Neglect* 30 (6): 657–77.

Sexual Offences Act. 2003. (c. 42).

Sheehy, E. A. 2012. *Sexual Assault in Canada: Law, Legal Practice, and Women's Activism*. Ottawa: University of Ottawa Press.

Sheppard, D., and P. Zangrillo. 1996. "Coordinating Investigations of Child Abuse." *Public Welfare* 54 (1): 21–28.

Simon, J. 2007. *Governing through Crime: How the War on Crime Transformed American Democracy and Created a Culture of Fear*. New York: Oxford University Press.

Simpson, R., J. Hughes, N. Slutskaya, and M. Balta. 2014. "Sacrifice and Distinction in Dirty Work: Men's Construction of Meaning in the Butcher Trade." *Work, Employment and Society* 28 (5): 754–70.

Slack, J. D. 1989. "Contextualizing Technology." In *Rethinking Communication*. Vol. 2, *Paradigm Exemplars*, edited by B. Dervin et al., 329–45. Newbury Park, CA: Sage.

Slack, J. D., D. J. Miller, and J. Doak. 1993. "The Technical Communicator as Author: Meaning, Power, Authority." *Journal of Business and Technical Communication* 7 (1): 12–36.

Slane, A. 2015. "Motion to Dismiss: Bias Crime, Online Communication, and the Sex Lives of Others in *NJ v. Ravi*." In *eGirls, eCitizens*, edited by J. Bailey and V. Steeves, 253–80. Ottawa: University of Ottawa Press.

Smart, C. 1989. *Feminism and the Power of Law*. New York: Routledge.

Sokoloff, N., and I. DuPont. 2005. "Domestic Violence and the Intersections of Race, Class, and Gender." *Violence against Women* 11 (1): 38–64.

Spencer, D. C., A. Dodge, R. Ricciardelli, and D. Ballucci. 2018. "'I Think It's Re-victimizing Victims Almost Every Time': Police Perceptions of Criminal Justice Responses to Sexual Violence." *Critical Criminology* 26 (2): 189–209.

———. 2021. "Emotional Labour, Police, and the Investigation of Sex Crimes Perpetrated against Children: Posttraumatic Stress and the Toll of Dirty Work." In *Handbook of Posttraumatic Stress: Psychosocial, Cultural, and Biological Perspectives*, edited by R. Ricciardelli, S. Bornstein, A. Hall, and R. N. Carleton. New York: Routledge.

Spencer, D. C., and J. Patterson. 2016. "Still Worlds Apart? Habitus, Field, and Masculinities in Victim and Police Interactions." In *Reconceptualizing Critical Victimology: Interventions and Possibilities*, edited by D. C. Spencer and S. Walklate, 15–31. Lanham, MD: Lexington Books.

Spencer, D. C., R. Ricciardelli, D. Ballucci, and K. Walby. 2019. "Cynicism, Dirty Work, and Policing Sex Crimes." *Policing: An International Journal* 43 (1): 151–65.

Spohn, C., and K. Tellis. 2012. "The Criminal Justice System's Response to Sexual Violence." *Violence against Women* 18 (2): 169–92.

Spohn, C., K. Tellis, and E. N. O'Neal. 2015. "Policing and Prosecuting Sexual Assault: Assessing the Pathways to Justice." In *Critical Issues on Violence against Women: International Perspectives and Promising Strategies*, edited by H. Johnson, B. S. Fisher, and V. Jaquier, 93–103. Global Issues in Crime and Justice 3. New York: Routledge.

Statistics Canada. 2014. *Police-Reported Sexual Offences against Children and Youth in Canada, 2012*. Ottawa: Government of Canada.

Strauss, A., and J. M. Corbin. 1997. *Grounded Theory in Practice*. Thousand Oaks, CA: Sage.

Tasca, M., N. Rodriguez, C. Spohn, and M. P. Koss. 2013. "Police Decision Making in Sexual Assault Cases: Predictors of Suspect Identification and Arrest." *Journal of Interpersonal Violence* 28 (6): 1157–77.

Title 18—Crimes and Criminal Procedure. Chapter 645. 1948.

Tonmyr, L., and A. Gonzalez. 2015. "Correlates of Joint Child Protection and Police Child Sexual Abuse Investigations: Results from the Canadian Incidence Study of Reported Child Abuse and Neglect—2008." *Health Promotion and Chronic Disease Prevention in Canada* 35 (8–9): 130–37.

Travis, L., and C. Winston. 1998. "Dissension in the Ranks: Officer Resistance to Community Policing, Cynicism, and Support for the Organization." *Journal of Crime and Justice* 21 (2): 139–56.

Tun, T., B. Price, A. Bandara, Y. Yu, and B. Nuseibeh. 2016. "Verifiable Limited Disclosure: Reporting and Handling Digital Evidence in Police Investigations." In *2016 IEEE 24th International Requirements Engineering Conference Workshops*, 102–5. Washington, DC: IEEE Computer Society.

Ullman, S. E., and S. M. Townsend. 2007. "Barriers to Working with Sexual Assault Survivors: A Qualitative Study of Rape Crisis Center Workers." *Violence against Women* 13 (4): 412–43.

Van Maanen, J. 1984. "Making Rank: Becoming an American Police Sergeant." *Urban Life* 13 (2): 155–76.

Virilio, P. 1991. *The Lost Dimension*. Translated by D. Moshenberg. Los Angeles, CA: Semiotext(e).

———. 2008. *Negative Horizon: An Essay in Dromoscopy.* Translated by M. Degener. London: Bloomsbury Academic.

Waddington, P. A. J. 1999. "Police (Canteen) Sub-culture: An Appreciation." *British Journal of Criminology* 39, no. 2 (Spring): 287–309.

Walklate, S. 2006. *Imagining the Victim of Crime*. London: Open University Press.

Walklate, S., J. Maher, J. McCulloch, K. Fitz-Gibbon, and K. Beavis. 2019. "Victim Stories and Victim Policy: Is There a Case for a Narrative Victimology?" *Crime, Media, Culture* 15 (2): 199–215.

Wall, D. S. 2007. "Policing Cybercrimes: Situating the Public Police in Networks of Security within Cyberspace." *Police Practice and Research* 8 (2): 183–205.

Wall, D. S., and M. Williams. 2007. "Policing Diversity in the Digital Age: Maintaining Order in Virtual Communities." *Criminology & Criminal Justice* 7 (4): 391–415.

Weiner, N. 1974. "The Effect of Education on Police Attitudes." *Journal of Criminal Justice* 2 (4): 317–28.

Wemmers, J. A. 2010. "The Meaning of Justice for Victims." In *International Handbook of Victimology*, edited by S. G. Shoham, P. Knepper, and M. Kett, 27–42. Boca Raton, FL: CRC Press.

Wenger, E. 2000. "Communities of Practice and Social Learning Systems." *Organization* 7 (2): 225–46.

Whatmore, S. 2006. "Materialist Returns: Practising Cultural Geography in and for a More-Than-Human World." *Cultural Geographies* 13 (4): 600–609.

Wise, J. M. 2005. "Assemblage." In *Gilles Deleuze: Key Concepts*, edited by C. J. Stivale, 77–87. Montreal, QC; Kingston, ON: McGill-Queen's University Press.

Worden, R. E. 1995. "Police Officers' Belief Systems: A Framework for Analysis." *American Journal of Police* 14 (1): 49–81.

World Health Organization. 2006. *Preventing Child Maltreatment: A Guide to Taking Action and Generating Evidence*. Geneva: WHO.

Yar, M. 2012. "E-Crime 2.0: The Criminological Landscape of New Social Media."
   Information & Communications Technology Law 21 (3): 207–19.
———. 2013a. "The Policing of Internet Sex Offences: Pluralized Governance versus Hierarchies of Standing." *Policing and Society* 23 (4): 482–97.
———. 2013b. *Cybercrime and Society*. 2nd ed. London: Sage.
Zahra, S. A., and G. George. 2002. "Absorptive Capacity: A Review,
   Reconceptualization, and Extension." *Academy of Management Review* 27 (2):
   185–203.

Index

About the Authors

Dale Spencer is associate professor and Faculty of Public Affairs' Research Excellence Chair in the Department of Law and Legal Studies at Carleton University in Ottawa, Ontario. Formerly a Banting Fellow and an Ontario Early Research Award recipient, Spencer has won the Faculty of Public Affairs Research Excellence Award and the Outstanding Faculty Graduate Mentor Award since arriving at Carleton in 2014. Spencer's main research interests are violence, sport, victimization, policing, youth, and conceptions of homelessness, domicile, and the law..

Rosemary Ricciardelli, PhD, is professor of sociology and criminology in the School of Maritime Studies and Research Chair in Safety, Security, and Wellness at Memorial University of Newfoundland's Fisheries and Marine Institute. She is the cochair of the Academic, Researcher, and Clinical Network Advisory Committee (ARC NAC) for the Canadian Institute for Public Safety Research and Treatment (CIPSRT). Beyond being elected to the Royal Society of Canada, Ricciardelli has additional affiliations and appointments at Ontario Shores Centre for Mental Health and Toronto Rehabilitation Institute. She has authored five edited collections and six monographs. Her research interests include gender, as well as experiences and issues within different facets of the criminal justice system. Her current research looks at prisons, desistance from crime, and the mental health and lived experiences of prisoners, prison officers, and police officers. Her sources of active research funding include Correctional Service Canada, the Social Sciences and Humanities Research Council of Canada, the Union of Canadian Correctional Officers (UCCO-SACC-CSN), the Union of Safety and Justice Employees (USJE), and the Canadian Institutes of Health Research (CIHR).

www.ingramcontent.com/pod-product-compliance
Lightning Source LLC
Chambersburg PA
CBHW021821270326
41932CB00007B/282